ADVANCE PRAISE FOR
START YOUR OWN HOME BUSINESS AFTER 50

"***Start Your Own Home Business After 50*** addresses the special needs, problems, and challenges of the over-50 entrepreneur who is looking to build an existing business or start a new one. Its guidance can help you create a successful home business that can generate an ongoing 'retirement annuity' for decades."
—**Robert Ringer**, bestselling author of *Winning Through Intimidation* and *Looking Out for Number One*

"If you're over 50 and you want to work from home, be your own boss, and control your own destiny, you must read this book. I have never read a book that so clearly provides a step-by-step road map to redefine your life and financial success and security. It's the single best resource I have ever seen on the topic."
—**Eric Yaverbaum**, bestselling author of six books including *Leadership Secrets of the World's Most Successful CEO's* and *PR For Dummies*

"If it's time to take your post-50 career into your own hands, ***Start Your Own Home Business After 50*** is an essential. It will give you realistic options for supporting yourself into retirement. Bob Bly knows from personal experience how to make the most of age and experience to succeed as an entrepreneur over 50. In this book, he lays out the options and points you in the right direction."
—**Ilise Benun**, Marketing-Mentor.com, author of seven books and co-producer of the Creative Freelancer Conference

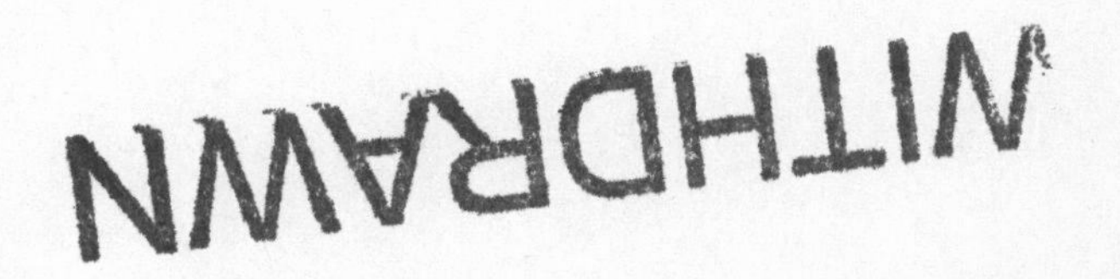

Start Your Own Home Business After 50

How to Survive, Thrive, and Earn the Income You Deserve!

Robert W. Bly

Fresno, California

Published by Quill Driver Books
An imprint of Linden Publishing
2006 South Mary Street, Fresno, California 93721
(559) 233-6633 / (800) 345-4447
QuillDriverBooks.com

Quill Driver Books and Colophon are trademarks of
Linden Publishing, Inc.

ISBN 978-1-61035-131-7

135798642

Printed in the United States of America
on acid-free paper.

Library of Congress Cataloging-in-Publication Data

Bly, Robert W.
Start your own home business after 50 : how to survive, thrive, and earn the income you deserve! / by Robert W. Bly.
pages cm
Includes bibliographical references and index.
ISBN 978-1-61035-131-7 (pbk. : alk. paper)
1. Home-based businesses--Management. 2. New business enterprises--Management. 3. Older people--Employment. I. Title.
HD62.38.B59 2013
658.1'1--dc23

2013000994

This book is for everyone over 50 who has started or is planning to start their own business.

Contents

Acknowledgments

I'd like to thank Kent Sorsky and Stephen Mettee for having faith in me and in this book. Thanks also to Nuritt Mittlefeldt for her invaluable research assistance. I'm also grateful to Frank Wilkinson, Amy Sprecher, and Tracy Minella for editorial contributions.

Introduction

You and I have never met, but if you are age 50 or over, I think I can guess a few things about you.

First, your primary financial goal at this point in life—aside from paying for your kids' college, if you haven't done so yet—is either (a) saving enough money between now and your retirement to retire comfortably or, if you are already retired, (b) making your money last for as long as you live.

Second, now that you are over 50, you are at a stage of your life where you are less interested in doing what others tell you to do and more interested in doing what you want to do, when and where you want to do it. You likely do not want to answer to a boss anymore, especially someone a lot younger than you.

Third, your degree of comfort with computers and technology, though possibly greater than mine, is most likely not equal to the average teenager's comfort with, and grasp of, today's technology. This point was driven home to me in a TV commercial for insurance from AARP. Teenagers today listen to music on iPods; the AARP commercial offered as a gift for responding an AM/FM radio—"old technology," as my 18-year-old son would call it.

Fourth, you are somewhat overwhelmed by the Internet. Every day you hear about some new gimmick for making money on the web. One day it's "tweeting." The next day you open a business magazine to an article saying every entrepreneur must have an RSS feed, a blog, online videos, or a Facebook page. You know nothing about any of them, and truth be told, none of them has much appeal to you.

Fifth, if you are over 50 and thinking of a new career, you are not alone. Every 7.5 seconds, another baby boomer in the United States reaches age 50, and they intend to keep working. According to the U.S. Department of Labor Statistics, the number of workers age 55 and over is projected to grow almost 47 percent by 2016.

Starting your own home-based business can help you with the first two problems described above, and, with *Start Your Own Home Business After 50* to guide you, the third and fourth problems won't in any way hinder your dream of starting your own business.

In fact, after reading *Start Your Own Home Business After 50*, you will be able to accomplish the following:

- Survive and thrive in a prolonged recession.
- Decide whether starting a home-based business right now is for you—and understand why working at home is so advantageous for over-50 entrepreneurs.
- Find a home business opportunity that can deliver the income and lifestyle you desire in your preretirement or retirement years.
- Generate an income stream or cash reserve from your new home business to replace what you may have lost in any of the recent stock market meltdowns or from no longer having a salary.
- Determine the target market (the types of customers) you want to reach.
- Create or source products and services that your target market needs, wants, and will buy.
- Effectively market and promote your product or service to attract new buyers.
- Generate repeat orders, referrals, and recurring revenues from existing customers.
- Set up and operate your new business from the comfort of your own home or apartment.
- Comply with laws, regulations, and codes governing the practice of your type of business.
- Generate enough income to quit your regular job and "retire" from the 9-to-5 corporate world for good—or earn enough money to supplement Social Security and other retirement income.

- Live off the income from your new business and leave your retirement nest egg entirely intact.
- Double your business by using the Internet to spread the word about your products and services and attract customers online.
- Increase your productivity and efficiency with the right hardware and software without having to become a techie.
- Create a business that does well enough to provide for you even during a recession or other economic or industry downturn.
- Set up a virtual company where assistants, vendors, and business partners all work off-premises and are connected to you by phone, fax, and Internet.

A research study I conducted on the over-50 generation (www.Marketing2Goms.com) found that older people place a priority on doing what they want to do vs. what someone tells them to do. That's no surprise. When you are a kid, you do what your parents and teachers tell you to do. As an adult, you are told what to do by your boss. By the time you are 50, you have been doing what others have told you to do for half a century. You're sick and tired of it. You want to be in control. If you have a full-time job, however, you aren't in control because other people tell you what to do and when to do it.

With your own home business, you call the shots. You are the boss. You make the decisions. You set your own hours. You choose who you will work with and how you'll spend your time, and you keep the bulk of the profits from the revenues you produce. Plus, with a laptop and wireless Internet connection, you can work where and when you want. No more being chained to a desk; you can run your business from your RV as you travel the country. You can sell products or perform services you're passionate about and earn an income that even an executive, doctor, or airline pilot might envy.

The bottom line: Following the advice in this book can take you from a job you don't enjoy and financial uncertainty to a career you love—as an entrepreneur following your dreams. You can learn how to earn in a few months what you now make in a year. If it happened to me, it can certainly happen to you, too. Let's get started…

1

The Over-50 Entrepreneur

"For many, achieving the American dream means taking control of their destiny, quitting their 9-to-5 job, and opening the doors to their very own business," writes Ed Hess in a July 2011 article in *SIPA Hotline*. These brave entrepreneurial souls have long shaped American enterprise, and today they're playing the very important role of helping to drive the nation's economic recovery. President Barack Obama has called small business the "backbone of our economy," as small businesses create two out of every three new jobs in America. About half of all Americans work for companies with fewer than 500 employees, and, according to the Small Business Administration, small business accounts for 50 percent of U.S. private, nonfarm, gross domestic product.

Yet, starting your own business at age 50 is a vastly different undertaking than starting a new business at age 20 or 30 or even 40. Over-50 entrepreneurs have many advantages compared with their younger counterparts, but they also face some disadvantages. This chapter will examine some of the pros and cons of starting a business after you have passed the half-century mark.

(Note: When I discuss the differences between being a 50- vs. a 30-year old entrepreneur, I must by necessity make generalizations, since I don't know you personally. So please, don't be offended if some of the descriptions don't quite fit you!)

Why is starting a business at age 50 so different than starting one when you are 20 years younger? There are several reasons, some of them positive and some of them negative. Let's lay out the advantages and the challenges in a table so you can visualize them easily before we examine them in detail below.

Entrepreneur at 50 vs. Entrepreneur at 30	
Your Challenges	**Your Advantages**
Lower energy level	More education
Lower enthusiasm	More life experiences
Possible health issues	More wisdom
Reluctance to embrace change	Increased ability to see the big picture

Disadvantages

Energy Level

Energy levels between different generations vary. For most of us, our mental and physical energy wanes gradually as we age. That's not to say that, at 54, I don't have plenty of energy for my two businesses: freelance copywriting—which I've done for decades—and Internet information marketing, which I started a few years ago. But my store of mental and physical energy now seems more finite. Many friends, acquaintances, and colleagues in my age group tell me that they too are beginning to slow down and need to take things easier.

When I was in my 30s and 40s, I routinely worked 12-hour days and absolutely enjoyed doing so, because I love what I do. I'm a workaholic—pity me. There was nothing I liked better than to sit at the keyboard, typing away writing copy for a client, or for a book, column, newsletter, or article.

I'm still actively working in both my freelance copywriting and my Internet businesses, but when I hit 50 or so, I felt my energy had been dialed down a notch. My days are more like nine or 10 hours, not 12, and on Fridays I peter out by about 4 or 5 P.M. I would still like to put in a 12-hour day if I could, but after about 10 hours, my concentration and mental energy fade to the point where I am no longer sufficiently productive to keep on going; that point used to come after about 12 to 13 hours.

I still get a lot more done in that time than most people I observe because I work in isolation; there is no one to shoot the breeze with and few distractions. And, I don't waste time on social media. Also, with three decades of experience, I know what I am doing and can therefore work efficiently. I included some of my time management secrets in a book, *Make Every Second Count: Time Management Tips and Techniques for More Success With Less Stress* (Career Press, 2010).

You may maintain peak energy well beyond 50, but at some point in your life—perhaps at 60, 70, or even 80—your mental and physical energy *will* start to decline. Your work hours will shorten, and you won't be quite as efficient and productive when you *are* working. As a result, you won't get quite as much done as when you were younger or achieve quite as much in a day as your younger competitors can achieve.

Enthusiasm Level

The next human characteristic to be affected by age is enthusiasm, or, rather, degree of enthusiasm.

How Bob Does It

What happens when you realize that you don't have the energy supply or reserves you did when you were younger? My advice is not to mourn it, as I initially did, but to accept this gradual decline in energy gracefully while taking steps to slow, halt, or—if you can—reverse it for a time. A regular program of exercise can give you more physical stamina and strength as well as make your mind sharper. There are also chemical means of gaining more energy.

I use a vitamin B_{12} oral spray when I need a shot of energy. It's safe, and vitamin B_{12} in liquid form is more rapidly absorbed than it is from a pill. One or two squirts under my tongue and I feel more refreshed and energetic.

Also, for better or for worse—I'm not a doctor, so I can't advise you here—I use caffeine as a way of boosting my energy. In my youth, when I worked in a corporate office, I didn't use the office coffeepot because I didn't drink coffee. But I noticed that my boss, 10 years older than me, couldn't start his day without it. Today, I can't get going in the morning without one or two cups of strong coffee. The second cup gradually cools off, and I sip the remaining cold coffee throughout the day until it's gone. Sometimes I pour a third cup.

While I haven't used them, there are a variety of energy drinks on the market today that may give you a boost, some with caffeine and some with vitamins, minerals, and herbs—and some with both. Sugar also gives people a shot of energy, but because I recently was diagnosed as prediabetic, sugar is not an option for me, though it may be for you. Be cautious, however. White, processed foods, such as sugar, salt, flour, and white bread, are not the healthiest foods for you.

People over 50 have a lot more accumulated life experience than entrepreneurs in their 30s. Decades of life experience can nurture a cynicism that makes a person cautious and wary; we've seen more than younger people, and done more, so we know that problems and pitfalls inevitably arise. By comparison, a 30-year-old may be *too* enthusiastic about a new business idea because he doesn't know the reality of what's possible versus what won't work. There are pros and cons to both vantage points.

A good illustration for me is writing a magazine article. I wrote my first magazine article in my 20s, and I will never forget the excitement of getting a copy of the magazine in the mail and seeing my byline in its pages. Now, 30 years later, I will write an occasional magazine article, and I enjoy doing it, but the thrill and excitement are gone; I've done it a hundred times already, so seeing my byline on article #101 just isn't an event for me anymore.

When you start a new business, you should—and really must—be enthusiastic about it, even excited. But you probably won't have the unbridled energy and excitement that a Generation X or Y entrepreneur would have. At this stage in my life, I can say that I enjoy my two businesses, but my excitement is fairly contained. I have a cynicism today I lacked as a younger man; it makes me wiser, but perhaps also dampens my enthusiasm a bit.

In many fields, especially science and technology, the major achievements are made by young men and women. Mark Zuckerberg, for example, founded Facebook while in his early 20s. Albert Einstein published his special theory of relativity when he was only 26.

Health Issues

Physical well-being—the degree of health and fitness you possess—invariably decreases with age. When you get older, you suddenly find yourself holding books away from your eyes so you can see the print clearly. You begin to keep a plastic case with daily pills in each compartment. You find yourself making a lot more trips to the pharmacy, as well as to your doctor. You wake up at night to pee. You have more aches and pains, and more concern about serious illnesses such as cancer and heart disease.

Taking care of and maintaining your own health becomes more time-consuming as you age, and those chores take time away from your new business. The majority of younger people are not burdened by health worries, so they are better able to concentrate on their business and spend more hours doing it without the interruption of a visit to the doctor's office or scheduling a chest x-ray.

I've had my share of health problems, and because I was so focused on my work, I ignored some of them—to my detriment. For instance, a few years ago, while I was on the telephone with a client, I became temporarily unable to speak or take notes with a pen. When these symptoms disappeared after a minute or so, I did the stupidest thing I ever did in my life: I ignored them and went back to work.

What I had was a TIA, or transient ischemic attack. A TIA, which is a temporary decrease of blood flow to the brain, is a warning sign of an impending stroke. If more men and women knew about and recognized TIA, thousands of needless strokes could be prevented. Later, I had a full-blown stroke. I recovered, but I still suffer from a slight loss of balance.

Reluctance to Embrace Change

When you're older, you become set in your ways. Your flexibility may diminish, and you may be less willing to accommodate others. This can be a problem, since you have to accommodate your customers and serve them in the manner they prefer. In my case, I have never liked gadgets or new technology, and, consequently, I don't own an iPhone, iPod, iPad, or wireless laptop.

This has disadvantaged me in some business meetings where clients take it as a matter of course that I should own these things and know how to use them. I had one meeting where everyone in the room was sending files back and forth between their various wireless devices, and I was embarrassed because I could not do so. My wife says I need to get with the times; no doubt she is right, but I am just set in my ways, and scoffing at what I consider newfangled toys is one of them.

I marvel at how young corporate men and women carry all these devices all the time and stay connected to business 24/7. Yes, it can be convenient, but surely it adds stress, too. At their age, they are able and willing to handle it. At 54, I am not. To always be connected electronically to work seems to be a burdensome thing.

Advantages

It's only smart to consider the possible disadvantages that come with advancing years and to make plans for how those issues will affect the way you do business. But don't let those issues scare you away! Entrepreneurs over 50 enjoy certain powerful advantages over the younger set.

More Education

Many of us with gray hair have much more education, both academic and on the job, than people decades younger. As a result, we know more. We have taken more courses and studied more subjects. And, although our degree may be old and our knowledge not always state of the art, our education includes not just college, but all the continuing education courses and at-work training seminars we have taken over the years.

More Life Experiences

The main advantages we over-50s have over our younger brethren are far more extensive experiences in life and in work. This greater experience, especially when combined with more schooling and training than the youngsters have, means that we simply know more, largely because we have faced and dealt with far more situations and problems than they have. Problems that are new and seemingly unsolvable to young people have already been faced and solved by their gray-haired counterparts.

In my day, younger people were more respectful of their elders; in the corporate world, we deferred to their more extensive knowledge and experience. Today, it is the opposite. We live in a culture that worships youth. Once you hit 50, it's extremely difficult to get hired, which is one reason why starting your own business is such an attractive option. In your own business, you can confidently put your knowledge and experience to work without having to prove anything to a boss who can't conceive of life without the Internet.

More Wisdom

All of your life experience makes you a wiser person. You know more because you have done more and seen more. Problems that seem insurmountable to the kiddies have already been faced and solved by their elders. We possess more common sense and can draw upon a much larger storehouse of experience. We are less impetuous and more deliberate and thoughtful. Ironically, although we have fewer years left to us, we act more slowly than young folks, who always seem in a terrible hurry. At least, that has been my experience.

"Wisdom is usually learned and earned through major experiences in life, both good and bad," writes Lauraine Snell in her book, *Start Your Own Business After 50 or 60 or 70* (Bristol Publishing, 1990).

Increased Ability to See the Big Picture

Snell lists additional reasons why the over-50 crowd has the advantage in starting a business.

- Older people were raised in an age where a strong work ethic was ingrained.
- Most people over 50 have been through multiple recessions, so they have learned how to survive tough times.
- Older people understand the principle of delayed gratification. They don't expect to make a million dollars or have dozens of customers their first year in business.
- Usually by sometime in our 50s, the children have gone off and we live in an empty nest, which means we can concentrate on our business without the distraction of raising kids.
- "Many beginning older business owners have already been successful in their lives as business owners, managers, or employees," writes Snell, "so they have greater business knowledge and a proven track record compared with younger entrepreneurs."

Financial Considerations

If you're over 50, you have more money issues to consider when starting a business than a younger person does. Many people in their 50s and older have considerable retirement savings, which could be a financial advantage to starting a business. They can afford to take some of this capital and invest it in a business, whereas 20- and 30-somethings are just starting out in life and have little or no savings.

If I wanted to launch a business with $100,000 start-up costs, I could do it without venture capital or loans. Yet, on the TV show *The Shark Tank*, you see people giving away 10 to 50 percent of their entrepreneurial ventures to investors who in exchange pay them relatively modest five-figure investments.

Of course, the flip side to that advantage is that those of us 50 and older also have to be more careful with our money. People in their 20s and 30s, many of whom are single and without children, can simply afford to take more risk than middle-aged folks, whether it's making investments or starting a business—even though they typically have less money. They can be more fearless, as they know that if their business tanks, there are still decades ahead to make up the loss and try again. Their peak earning years are either at hand or still ahead of them, and when you are 20 or 30, you think you are immortal.

For those of us in our fifties or older, we are approaching retirement age, even if it's not in the immediate future. We are past our peak earning years, yet with retirement approaching, our need for cash may be great. Therefore, we must be conservative with our money and investments. We cannot afford to risk it all on an uncertain business venture, and some of us may not be willing to give up the security of a 9-to-5 salary for the uncertainty of self-employment.

In March 2009, the financial crisis sent U.S. stocks to a 13-year low. Investors gave back $7 trillion in wealth and lost 22 percent of their retirement savings—adding to the degree of financial uncertainty for those at or near retirement age—forcing some folks to delay their retirement for years. A recent survey by the Employee Benefit Research Institute found that only 23 percent of workers plan to retire before age 65, down from 50 percent in 1991.

You're probably going to live longer than your parents and grandparents did. Over the past 100 years, the life expectancy at birth has gone up 28 years, from 49 to 77 years of age, so it's more difficult than ever to accumulate enough money in a traditional IRA to make sure you don't outlive your retirement savings. But if you own your own business and set your own working hours and retirement age, you may also be able to count on more working years to accumulate those savings.

According to *Kiplinger's Personal Finance*, you need at least a million dollars to retire these days. Most Americans don't have anywhere near that: The average retirement account balance in the United States for men and women ages 55 to 69 is a mere $42,500.

But even if you do have a million dollars, stock market crashes, cyclical bear markets, and inflation can quickly eat into your retirement nest egg. Some experts now say you need two or three million to retire comfortably.

No wonder 95 percent of Americans rely on Social Security or other government programs to help them keep a roof over their heads during retirement! But when you have your own profitable business, you don't have to rely on family members or Uncle Sam for support. You remain financially independent, able to support yourself in the lifestyle to which you have become accustomed.

What Brings You to This Decision?

Let's talk a bit about how you have made the decision to start a home-based business. If you've just retired and are now living on a pension, Social Security, or investments, that gives you some income on a continual basis, which is a big plus. That steady income gives you breathing time to put your business together without the pressure of finding money fast.

Others of you may have come to this decision because you were laid off or fired, or you have some other reason for needing to start an income-producing business quickly. In this case, you will probably need to move more quickly in setting up your business and won't have the luxury of easing your way into the transition.

Word to the Wise: Claim Unemployment

For those of you who just got fired or laid off, possibly because of your age, things will be a little rough if you do not have enough money put aside to live on for a few months until you get your business rolling. If that is the case, go online to file for unemployment immediately. If you get laid off today, file tomorrow. Every day you delay in filing your claim, you will lose that day's money if you do get approved.

If you don't get approved, then fight the decision. You will be notified about participating in a phone interview concerning what happened to you, and you will need to stand up for yourself and define the good job you were doing, particularly if you can show documentation to your interviewer. Your interviewer has the authority to override the employer and charge their account for money due to you. How you present yourself and your case makes the difference in their decision. Be firm, accurate, and do not insult your former employer to the interviewer. Just be sure to get your point across.

Once approved, it takes a full month before you see your first unemployment paycheck, but then you will receive several back paychecks, which will help enormously. But, until then, you will have a month to suffer until that payment comes in. Every state handles the unemployment process differently, so it is up to you to find out what to do and how to do it. Do not feel guilty about accepting unemployment insurance: It's your tax money.

No matter which route you've taken to the decision to start your own home-based business, most likely you are feeling that there has to be more to life; that you want to live a richer, fuller life, and that you want to be in control of what happens to you. You're tired of bosses who run you around and tell you to do things that really don't make sense and are not efficient in accomplishing your work. Not only that, but the threat of being fired or laid off without any input is humiliating and degrading.

After age 50, the threat of being fired looms especially large, since employers often are prejudiced against older workers and prefer to hire younger people. Therefore, if you lose your 9-to-5 job, it is difficult to find another. Setting up your own business may be a more viable option than looking for another job, since age doesn't matter and you won't have to answer to anyone else.

Being a business owner changes your whole mindset. While there is fear of the unknown, it is still a liberating feeling to think you can be in control of making your own money while doing work that you enjoy—and you can do so for the rest of your life, if you so choose. It is not an easy path, especially in the beginning when you are trying to put it all together. There does come the day, however, when you can finally take that vacation you've always wanted, or buy that car or house you've dreamed about.

How This Book Can Help

In the chapters ahead, you will find some ideas for home-based businesses that could bring you the kind of schedule and financial freedom you have only dreamed of. You will learn about businesses such as freelancing, coaching, Internet marketing, and selling imports and exports, among others.

These are not get-rich-quick schemes but real businesses that will require hard work, planning, and organization to make them succeed. To help you, this book provides ideas about how to set up your business, organize your home office, market your services, and operate as a virtual company.

You've spent decades working for someone else; let the information in this book help you strike out on a new path. It's not too late.

STRAIGHT TALK FROM BOB

What's scarier than starting your own business?

In my opinion, it's having a 9-to-5 job!

What makes me say so?

Well, there has been a huge "paradigm shift" (forgive the jargon) in employment that has turned the work world upside down. When I was a young lad fresh out of college in the late '70s, getting a corporate job—like I did—was the safe, secure thing to do.

Entrepreneurs, by comparison, were seen as crazy risk-takers—gambling their futures on uncertain ventures.

Today, it's quite the opposite.

By starting their own companies, entrepreneurs take control of their work life. They protect themselves from pink slips by being business owners, because they are their own bosses. Meanwhile, the 9-to-5 world has become a shaky and uncertain place. The old "guaranteed" job security of the 1970s is gone.

So, what can you do about it now? If you are in your 50s or 60s, you are easing toward retirement or perhaps you're already retired. Or, maybe you've been downsized—or even pushed out by a company after you've given it decades of your best work. Starting a home-based business can provide the extra income you need to live on now and fill your coffers so that you can achieve your retirement investing goal.

If you are in your 70s, 80s, and beyond, you are almost certainly retired from full-time work, which usually means you no longer have much income outside of Social Security or pensions. You may be living more frugally than you'd like. Operating your own small business can put thousands of dollars of extra cash into your pocket to supplement your pension and Social Security.

Regardless of age, there are very few of us in today's economy who couldn't use more money. Launching your own small business is one of the surest ways to earn the extra income you need.

2

Home-Based Business Opportunity #1: Freelancing

By the time we've reached 50, most of us have been through the wringer several times in life, so we have plenty of experience we can share with other people about what to do, how to act, and how to run a business. If you've worked for others over your lifetime, surely you've run across a boss or two who just didn't get it when it came to running a business or who couldn't keep repeat customers—let alone loyal employees. You also know tons about customer service and business operations and best practices, in part from having observed the mistakes others made. So, how about parlaying that experience, or portions of it, into a business all your own? Now you can be your own boss and have fun doing it.

In fact, it doesn't matter if you've spent many years in one type of business or if you've been involved in several businesses and careers over your life. You can always find a way to create a home-based business as a freelancer based upon those experiences.

Then again, maybe you don't want to revisit any of those former jobs or professions. Instead, you have a hobby that you would love to develop into an expert-level gig and make money with your expertise. So, go ahead, build a business around it, and enjoy doing what you love most. You've got a whole new life ahead of you!

What Can You Do?

You can work as a freelancer in many different fields. The following list should give you some ideas:

- Accountant
- Architect

- Attorney
- Blogger
- Computer programmer
- Contractor
- Copywriter
- Desktop publisher
- Editor
- Graphic designer
- Illustrator
- Journalist
- Linguist
- Magazine article writer
- Photographer
- Project manager
- Researcher
- Social networker
- Statistician
- Videographer
- Web designer
- Web marketer

Is This for Me?

It's pretty easy to hang out your shingle as a freelancer. But don't just jump right in without thinking a few things through. Before you actually start freelancing, you need to attend to a few planning issues. First, plan out what you want to do, then create a marketing plan and a business plan, set goals, arrange your financial setup with a bank for the money you'll make as a freelancer, and determine what tools you'll need to accomplish all of those steps.

Even if you do jump in and get rolling with clients right away, the business side of your business must be tended to fairly quickly, including creating nuts-and-bolts items such as the first invoice or written agreement. At the very least, start with the basics of your business and a solid marketing plan; you will be developing these more fully over time. Look for more information about developing business and marketing plans in chapters 10 and 12 of this book, and check out my 2010 book, *The Marketing Plan Handbook* from Entrepreneur Press, for even more details.

As a freelancer and your own boss, you are totally responsible for your business—its success or failure—and for your self-motivation to that end. If you have enough operational structure set up in advance, it's easier to create goals and motivate yourself on a daily basis because your foundation is already set. So start building your foundation by first determining *what* you want to do. Knowing what kind of business you want to run can help you determine what steps to take next to build on that foundation.

Deciding What Business You Want

So now you know you want to freelance, but you're not sure exactly what it is you want to do. Start first by making a list (or go through your résumé) of what jobs you have held, and what responsibilities you have had, and think about whether you might want to offer your services on a freelance basis to former bosses or if you just want to start out fresh looking for new clients. Generally, it's easier to start by working with former bosses who know you and who respect the work you've done in the past. They, in turn, can pass you on to some of their associates or clients, or perhaps provide referrals to other people who might be interested in your services. This is word-of-mouth marketing and public relations at its best and cheapest.

Word to the Wise

Don't burn your bridges with former bosses, even ones you didn't particularly enjoy working with. You may have hated working for them at the office, but they might be much easier to deal with if you are a freelance consultant instead of their employee. Who knows? One of your least-favorite bosses just might turn out to be your golden ticket to fast-track freelancing.

Back to that list you made of jobs you've held: There may be a job or two on the list that you really enjoyed but don't feel you could perform well as a freelancer; however, perhaps some small aspect of even those jobs could be developed as an outsource opportunity for you. Let's consider two small ideas.

Project Summaries

Let's say you spent years as a market researcher and analyst for a large company. Now, you could use that experience to write project summaries. You could set up an arrangement with your former employer—or a new client—so that they send their data to you with a summary of the desired project and pay you to write a report, summary, or analysis based on the information. Not only could you write reports, but you could also create tables, spreadsheets with pivot tables and analysis, graphs, and whatever else you need to show your interpretation of the data. Just be sure that any analysis and macros you create for such projects have been double- or even triple-checked and tested thoroughly. Numbers and statistics must be accurate.

All information pertaining to that client is confidential, and you can never show it to anyone else unless it's years later and the company has closed down. Even then, think twice about it. If you want to present a sample of your work, you can re-create a presentation with a fictional product and revised data throughout the report. Remove company logos and names, of course, and make the examples all your own.

Online Surveys

You can also think about creating online surveys for companies, especially those in your specialty area, who want to know more about what their customers think about the products they buy or services they use. There are many online survey companies you can use to develop specialized surveys for just about any kind of business that needs your help. Once the survey is done, you can collect the data and, depending on the objective of the survey, create a presentation report based on that information.

You can do this kind of work for just about any type of business, but you definitely need a good consultation with a client company contact who has a definitive idea about what the company wants to find out from this survey. You may need to do several revisions as the survey is developed. Also, be sure that you have only one established contact for the survey information. Trying to put together a survey while consulting with four or five people who each call you with their own ideas about how it should be done is a royal nightmare. Nip that situation in the bud and establish one contact only, and put the goals of the project in writing.

Survey Monkey (at www.SurveyMonkey.com) is one place to start looking at how surveys are created and how the data is presented to you at the close of the survey. You can sign up for free just to get an idea of how things work, but be aware that the free version limits the amount of questions per survey and how many users can take the survey. Still, it is a good way to start.

If you get into surveys as part of your business services, either through surveying your own clients, or creating them for other businesses and their products and services, definitely consider using the upgrades at Survey Monkey that allow many more options for you to work with and also give your work a more professional look. Once you have an understanding of online surveys, you can look at other survey companies to see what services they provide and whether they can offer you a better deal, based on what kind of returns you want to get.

How Bob Does It

Anyone who is setting up a freelance business has to figure out how to find clients. When I started freelancing full-time in February 1982, there was no Internet, and "networking" was something you did face-to-face.

My main way of getting clients back then was to send out postal mail—sales letters promoting my copywriting services. It worked incredibly well. Then I started to add other marketing tools, such as writing articles and giving talks, which also worked well.

Today, a lot of my clients come from the Internet, specifically from my search-optimized copywriting website, www.bly.com, and from my e-newsletter, which has 65,000 subscribers. I also still give talks, which are another effective way of drumming up business.

If a person who contacts me doesn't have a company name or her own website, I dismiss the inquiry as not serious. I also turn away anyone who says something like, "We have a small budget." If they can't afford me, they can't have me.

For many more tips, read my book *Selling Your Services: Proven Strategies for Getting Clients to Hire You (or Your Firm)* (Henry Holt, 1992).

Planning Is Key

Of course, writing reports or creating surveys are not the only ways you can turn your past jobs into a freelance career. But you get the idea. Examine your jobs and the skills you gained in your years at work to see how you can turn that experience into your very own freelance business, one which you enjoy and find fulfilling. Obviously, if you didn't enjoy a particular type of work, don't try to do it as a freelancer. Believe me, your clients will know it when they see the work you provide them.

That's the key to planning what you want to do as a freelance business: Do something you're good at and that you enjoy doing. Your enthusiasm will impress potential clients when they are first trying to decide whether to hire you. Make sure that your enthusiasm is geared to your clients and their needs. It's not about you; it's about what's in it for them if they hire you. Therefore, to get a clear idea about what you want to do, make that list of each previous job and what skills you learned during the course of each job.

Having a Vision

Once you have an idea of what you want to do, spend some time thinking about how you want to do it and what a successful business will look like. What will you offer as a freelancer that a potential employer couldn't find among his own employees? Who will you market your services to that other freelancers in your field might be overlooking? What will your business look like one year from now? How about five years from now?

Having a vision of your business allows you to determine how you will make your service or product better than most others on the market, and it will help you decide how detailed your plans need to be when you are getting started. You can say to yourself that you want to freelance so you can be your own boss and take vacations whenever you want, but to make that happen, you have to create a *successful* business. And the way to build a successful business is by focusing on what benefits and features you will be providing to clients. For your business to be successful, everything needs to be directed to your customers, especially if you want repeat business.

A home-based freelance business can be incredibly simple or highly complex. If your previous job included computer programming, for example, you could choose to tutor local high school students one-on-one in your home so that they can learn simple skills. Or, you could choose to create intricate programs that address problems common to a particular field and then market those programs to multinational corporations around the world.

If you use your imagination AND do your homework, you can soon be thriving in a business you thoroughly enjoy.

STRAIGHT TALK FROM BOB

One day, my wife, my oldest son, and I went to a beautiful little stable in Pennsylvania so we could ride horses.

Well, they rode the horses. I declined. The truth is I am not crazy about horses.

So, while they rode for an hour, I sat outside at a picnic table and read my favorite publication, the *New York Review of Books*. It was a beautiful autumn day. I was surrounded by hills with an explosion of trees decorated green, brown, yellow, orange, and red.

After their ride, my wife and son told me, "You really missed out on all the fun."

That's what they thought, but I didn't think I had missed out on anything. I did what I wanted to do, and I really enjoyed myself.

You shouldn't do what others think you should do just to make them happy. You should do what you want to do to make yourself happy.

When I graduated from college, I took a corporate job, which pleased my father to no end. In his mind, it paid a steady salary and was safe and secure. But I was bored. So I became a freelance writer.

He felt I was making a mistake, giving up my safe and secure corporate job and my steady salary. Early on in my freelancing, I did a large job for a software company and got a check for $10,000 (that was a lot of money in the early 1980s).

Wisely, I copied the check and showed it to my father. He never again complained about me quitting my corporate job.

Make yourself happy. When you do, those who care about you will eventually be happy for you.

3

Home-Based Business Opportunity #2: Consulting

Consulting is an ideal home business for over-50, white-collar professionals. How is it different from freelancing? There are several ways, but the key one is this: Freelancers perform particular jobs or tasks; consultants tell *other* people how to perform particular jobs or tasks in order to attain desired outcomes.

Let us delve into the reasons why, at this stage in your life, you might decide to become a consultant. Chances are you fall into one of the following three scenarios, or a combination thereof:

- **Scenario I.** You have voluntarily retired and are looking for a way to remain socially and mentally active, as well as supplement your income.
- **Scenario II.** You have re-evaluated your life and want to earn a living doing something that is both intellectually and personally satisfying.
- **Scenario III.** You were laid off or forced into early retirement, leaving you needing money to pay the bills.

The one common factor in each of these scenarios is MONEY. You want or need to earn some money. There is no question that consulting is a way to make money, but you first must establish income goals and a plan for achieving those goals.

At this stage in your life, you probably are not looking to become rich. If unimaginable wealth is a consequence of your consulting endeavors, you probably will not shun it, but it is not your overarching goal. More likely, your goal is to earn enough money to do one or more of the following things:

- Maintain your current lifestyle
- Build an inheritance or college fund for your children and grandchildren
- Finance special projects like kitchen remodeling or a vacation abroad
- Build up your retirement nest egg
- Purchase a second home or new car

Set an Income Goal

Whatever the reason you want or need money, you should be able to articulate a specific dollar figure as your total annual income goal. A realistic annual income target is one that you can attain within a few years.

In determining your annual income goal, you should start with the amount of money you need to live comfortably for a year. Then, double it. So, if your annual living expenses total about $30,000 per year, your annual income goal should be $60,000.

Does this sound ambitious to you? Well, it is ambitious, but it is also achievable. Many consultants earn $100,000 to $250,000 or more. Also, if you are receiving Social Security or retirement benefits, part of your annual income goal has already been met, reducing the money you need to make from your consulting business.

Establish Your Rates

Knowing your annual income goal is essential to establishing your fees and setting your compensation rates for your consulting services. If you know how much you need to make, it is easier to determine what you need to charge for your services.

Novice and even experienced consultants sometimes find themselves struggling to determine the amount they should charge for their products and services. If you approach this issue believing that you, with all of your business and life experience, add value, then it makes determining your own rates that much easier.

The dilemma arises from the need to strike a balance between charging enough to maximize the demand for your services so you can make this endeavor financially worthwhile and not charging so much that you lose out on jobs to other consultants. Many consultants, especially novices, charge too little at the beginning in the hopes of getting the job, and then they become resentful when they realize they are doing too much work for too little compensation. Yet they are afraid to charge higher prices for fear the potential client will object, saying "Your price is too high."

There are other factors to consider as well. Unlike when you worked for a company, you will now be footing the bills for all aspects of your business, such as overhead, labor, cost of materials, and profit margin. There are also intangible factors. For instance, if you are the cheapest consultant in town, you may be erroneously viewed as less experienced or less skilled. You may be conveying a message that your expertise is so inexpensive because you are not as good as the more expensive consultants.

How Bob Does It

A sign on the shop floor of a manufacturing facility showed a triangle. Each corner was labeled: One was GOOD, another was FAST, the third was CHEAP. The caption under the triangle said PICK ANY TWO.

It makes sense to me. If you are cheap and fast, you probably aren't very good. If you are good and fast, you can and should charge a premium fee. If you are cheap and good, you probably have more customers than you can handle.

If you are all three—cheap, good, fast—you are under constant pressure and probably not making that much money.

Which are you—good, fast, or cheap?

Is This for Me?

By the time you reach your 50s, you have learned quite a few things through hard work, by chance, and through trial and error. And, while the journey has been mostly splendid, you now stand at a crossroads, either by choice or by circumstance, about your next career move. Ideally, you would like to expend your energy on something worthwhile and lucrative. However, what you do not want—and cannot afford—to do is to spend the next decade trying to figure out what that something is and how to do it. So, the first step is to determine if the consulting profession is a good fit for you.

The standard *Webster's* dictionary definition of a consultant is "one who gives professional advice or services; expert." In practical terms, if you are in the business of consulting, then you are in the business of sharing what you know with others—whether individuals or corporate entities—for the purposes of assisting and facilitating the achievement of some personal or business goal or objective.

You should carefully weigh some basic elements of being a consultant before hanging your shingle on the door. These elements apply regardless of the type of consulting service you decide to offer. This is a very important step, because a careful and honest assessment of the pros and cons of starting a consulting business could have a direct impact on your ultimate success and personal satisfaction.

Entrepreneurial Spirit

An independent consultant is an entrepreneur, and being an entrepreneur involves risks, long hours, independence, self-determination, and, in some cases, isolation. Virtually all successful entrepreneurs possess at least some of the same characteristics. According to an article in *SAP Connection*, Terri Lonier, author of *Working Solo*, says that successful solo entrepreneurs are self-starters, outgoing, life-long learners, and optimistic. An article in Volume 8 of the newsletter *Creative Business* (www.CreativeBusiness.com) describes solo and small-firm practitioners as people who:

- Enjoy working at home alone
- Are somewhat motivated by money
- Are not that interested in business details
- Do not want to supervise others

Yet another characteristic of entrepreneurs is that they are self-starters who are fully capable of doing work without being told to do it, supervised, or otherwise having their hand held.

Is this you? Do you have the entrepreneurial spirit? Can you sustain it?

If you have spent the bulk of your career in a corporate or corporate-like environment, transitioning to entrepreneurship can be frightening, even if you currently have no other options. For many of us, working for and reporting to someone else is the natural order of things, and we have no desire to be burdened with the administrative minutia and networking that comes along with running your own shop.

Moreover, in the corporate environment, whether you have some, little, or no work to do, you will still get paid your salary and receive your benefits. This is not the case for the self-employed. A "sick day" can ruin your bottom line. When you are an entrepreneur, if you do not work, you do not get paid.

Even if you never take a sick day in your life, economic downturns can have an adverse effect on your consulting business. When companies are forced to cut costs, the "consultant" is usually the first to go. Growth in some consulting specialties, such as executive search consulting, is directly tied to the health of the industries in which they operate. If the industry in which you have expertise fades, so do your consulting opportunities.

On the other hand, depending upon the service that you offer, a recession may be the ticket to success for your consulting business, as companies consider means to simultaneously cut costs and remain competitive by relying on consultants to handle some of their work. Consultants tend to cost a company less than a full-time employee, and if the company needs to develop a survival strategy during trying economic times, it often will seek the advice of consultants on the best way to do so.

Need for Socializing

Being a consultant can be a solitary existence. Although you will be working and making decisions for yourself, which is a prime benefit of entrepreneurship, you will also, most likely, be by yourself most of the time. If you are an introvert, with no special desire to be near or around other people, you will love this part of being a consultant. If you are an extrovert, however, this may be difficult.

Some of your best friends may be former workplace colleagues, but do not expect to make such friendships as a consultant. Consulting gigs rarely last forever, and, as such, you will not often have the opportunity to cultivate and nurture meaningful relationships or connections with your colleagues. As esoteric as this may sound, it is actually the largest complaint among long-time consultants. According to an article in the *New York Daily News*, when asked what they miss most about the corporate world, 68 percent of entrepreneurs interviewed cited office socializing.

Self-Determination and Financial Prosperity

The most compelling upside to being an independent consultant is that you will be able to do work you actually like and enjoy doing most of the time. Imagine that: getting up every morning to perform tasks and jobs that stimulate and excite you. This factor alone can generate a successful consulting endeavor.

Sales trainer Paul Karasik observes, "What motivates people is doing what they love." Furthermore, in an issue of *Words from Woody*, David Wood quotes Michael Korda as saying, "Your chances of success are directly proportional to the degree of pleasure you derive from what you do."

A related and equally compelling benefit of being an independent consultant is the ability to control your own destiny on matters ranging from job assignments to taking care of personal matters, such as caring for children or elderly parents, without the threat of negative performance reviews. Self-determination is a keen motivator, and, for many, it is well worth the risk of starting an entrepreneurial endeavor.

Yet another positive and extremely relevant aspect of being an independent consultant is money. Consulting presents an opportunity to make more money than you probably did as a traditional employee. Many consultants have reported earning two or three times as much money consulting than they did working as a corporate employee. Just remember, this prosperity is strongly influenced by market conditions and your willingness to work hard to promote yourself.

Demand and Competition

You can have confidence in the fact that the market demand for consultants is diverse and ever present. Clients are always searching for the "secret" formula for starting and maintaining a successful and profitable business, and they hope consultants can provide them with that recipe.

For this reason, no matter the industry, start-up and established companies will seek out consultants to provide guidance on drafting business plans and budgets; developing strategy, logistics, security, and information technology (IT); and to keep them updated on municipal, state, and federal laws that may impact the bottom line.

There are, however, two important caveats. So be aware!

First, because there is a demand, the competition can be fierce. Everybody wants a piece of the consulting pie. Moreover, consulting is not a complex concept. In fact, anyone who has specialized knowledge, the ability to communicate clearly, and a willingness to work hard can call themselves a consultant. Many people do just that.

Consulting is the fastest-growing and one of the highest-paying labor sectors in the country. Competition for consulting jobs is keen; only the most educated and experienced workers will have the best job prospects, and only about 21 percent of all consultants are self-employed, so you will need to be prepared to work really hard to succeed. And, if working hard scares you, then this is definitely not the road you want to take.

Second, with the exception of highly specialized consulting services, like chemical engineering, the demand for the consulting services that you offer is driven not only by economic growth, but also by whether the current market trends actually demonstrate a need for your type of expertise and knowledge.

As stated earlier, during an economic boom, most companies will have little use for consulting expertise about surviving a recession. And, for those companies that do require reorganization/survival strategies during an otherwise great economic market, you can expect that you will have to pursue any opportunities for those jobs very aggressively, to stand out from the competition.

Although there is no guaranteed formula for success, it is possible to overcome and defy the obstacles that you encounter, using hard and intelligent work and a healthy dose of tenacity and determination.

So, you need to ask yourself, at this stage in your life, are you ready to work really hard? If the answer is yes, then the possibilities are limitless.

Word to the Wise

You must remember this and never forget it: ***Your skills, knowledge, and experience are valuable.*** At your age, you have acquired decades of business and/or life experience that even the most intelligent 20- or 30-something consultant cannot come close to. Unlike younger consultants, you possess the maturity that comes from having lived life; that experience cannot be obtained by doing a search on the Internet.

A Self-Assessment Test

Let's play a game of 20 Questions. Answer the questions below. The more honest "yes" answers you score, the stronger your aptitude and desire to become an independent consultant ("no" answers suggest the opposite):

- Do you like solving problems?
- Do you enjoy research, study, and learning?
- Are you an "information junkie"—subscribing to newsletters, clipping articles, and collecting tidbits and facts on subjects that interest you?
- Are you a self-starter? Can you work independently without a boss to tell you what to do or without the constant interaction you get in an office environment?
- Do you have specialized skills, knowledge, and/or experience that's in demand?
- Do businesses or individuals regularly hire consultants in your area of specialty?
- Would businesses or individuals profit or otherwise benefit by engaging your services?
- Can you achieve results for consulting clients that can be measured, documented, and proven?
- Is the service you can offer unique, different, or better than similar services being offered elsewhere?
- If not, is there another compelling reason why clients should hire you instead of your competitors?
- Can you charge an hourly rate that is equivalent to at least twice your current salary as a corporate employee?
- Can you get along with people well enough to sell your services and deal with clients?
- If you are not comfortable with people, can you find someone who can do these things for you, allowing you to concentrate on the technical side of your business?

- Do you have the fortitude to handle crises and other business problems?
- Do you have money in the bank you can live on for a few months if business gets lean?
- Are you flexible and accommodating, and willing to listen to the requirements and opinions of other people—specifically, your customers?
- Are you results oriented?
- Can you commit to and meet deadlines without procrastination or excuses?
- Would you enjoy working at home or alone in a small office?
- Do you have good computer skills and, if not, are you willing to learn them?

Identify Your Marketable Skills, Knowledge, or Experience

So, now that you are of aware of the risks, benefits, and immense satisfaction that comes along with being a consultant, do you believe that this is, indeed, a career move worth exploring? If so, then the next critical step on this journey is to identify that combination of skill, knowledge, and experience you possess that you can base your consulting business on. In other words, it is time to identify exactly what you bring to the table.

When you are 50 or older, this particular step can be far less daunting than it is for people in their 20s, 30s, and even 40s. By this time in your life, you have a full armory of knowledge and skills that you have spent a lifetime acquiring. Unlike your younger counterparts, you can have confidence that you have seen it all and know what works and what does not.

Essentially, you can consult about anything that you have experience doing and/or do well. However, you need to ask yourself this question: Is that knowledge or experience marketable? Is there a need for the type of skills, knowledge, and experience that I have to offer? Will somebody else find what I know or do to be valuable enough to pay me for it?

The range of marketable skills, experience, and knowledge is vast. Some of the most commonly marketed consulting services are described below.

This is by no means a comprehensive list, but it does represent the type of expertise most often offered by consultants.

Management consultant. A management consultant has experience in almost every aspect of corporate operations: marketing, finance, corporate strategy and organization, manufacturing processes, information systems and data processing, e-commerce or business, and human resources, including benefits and compensation. As a general matter, the fundamental skill of a management consultant is the ability to study and analyze business-related problems—typically by synthesizing information from many sources—and then recommend solutions to those problems.

Administrative consultant. Administrative consultants possess general and specialized expertise in a broad range of office-related areas. Specifically, an administrative consultant can provide advice and counsel about office management, administrative processes, administrative support needs, requirements and standards, bookkeeping, audits, and accounting.

Occupational safety consultant. Occupational safety consultants provide expert guidance in identifying workplace safety hazards and ensuring that employers are in compliance with government worker safety regulations. They also have knowledge and experience in planning a safe and healthy environment for workers, identifying hazardous materials or systems that may cause illness or injury, assessing safety risks associated with machinery, investigating accidents, and assessing legal vulnerabilities due to safety code violations.

Information technology (IT) consultants. IT consultants, who in this information age are always in demand, provide both general and highly specialized services. Some IT consultants provide general computer troubleshooting services or database management, while others have experience and skill in designing and developing new hardware and software systems.

Marketing and communications consultants. A marketing and/or communications consultant provides assistance in areas ranging from product development to public relations and customer service. This type of consultant typically has extensive writing or other media experience, such as graphic design, website content and design, and so on.

Scientific and technical consultants. Scientific and/or technical consultants possess skills, knowledge, and expertise that is typically highly specialized. As a general matter, these types of consultants advise on issues relating to physical (agriculture, physics, chemistry, biology) and social (law, economics, environment) sciences. In many ways, they are like management consultants. Although their services do not relate to management in the traditional sense, the advice or findings of a scientific or technical consultant can and do impact critical management decisions about operations, organizational structure, and overall operational decisions—typically from the perspective of avoiding liability or boosting profit margins.

SECURITY CONSULTANT. Security consultants provide advice on how to ensure the safety and security of an organization's physical and human assets that may be threatened by natural or human-made disasters, terrorism, vandalism, and theft. Security consultants also provide guidance on developing emergency evacuation procedures or measures to minimize structural damage done to a building during a hurricane, earthquake or some other catastrophic event.

MIND THE GAPS

The range of consulting possibilities is, quite literally, endless. Today, we live in an age of specialization. More information has been created in the past 30 years than in the previous 5,000. As a result, there is no way any single individual can know all there is to know about everything, so naturally outside help and expertise is sought to fill the knowledge gap. That is why consultants exist—to fill in the gaps. Your task is to figure out (1) what you know and do well and (2) if (and how) you can market your knowledge and skills.

"So," you ask, scratching your head, "how do I do that?"

A good place to start is to list all the areas in which you feel you have significant and substantive skills, knowledge, and/or expertise. In making this list, do NOT limit yourself to those areas of expertise or skills that are derived from your job. The list should also include those things that you just naturally excel at doing.

For example, if you know everything there is to know about computer systems because that has been the focus of your entire professional career, all the skills associated with that knowledge should definitely be a part of your list. However, if you also possess a talent for developing systems to keep people organized in their daily lives at home and at work, then this skill also deserves to be on your list.

Rank Your Skills

Once your list is complete, go back through the items and indicate your range of expertise in each of these areas on a scale from 1–10. A 10 indicates that no one can address this task better than you, while a 1 means that you could probably use a consultant yourself to help you hone this skill. Now, go back through the list again and eliminate any item that falls below 7.

If you still have more than 10 items, go back through the list and again numerically rank what is left. Your goal is to narrow down the list to your top five items. Once you have a five-item list, assign a number of 1–5 to indicate which area of expertise gives you the most personal satisfaction. Remember the quote from sales trainer Paul Karasik: "What motivates people is doing what they love." When you are a consultant, you can make money by practicing your favorite skill or dealing with the subjects that interest you most. Assigning a 5 to an item means that an area satisfies you very much, while a 1 means that you may like working in that area, but you don't love it.

So, now you have determined not only your top areas of expertise, but also which areas and tasks you most enjoy. Your next step is to assess what you offer in terms of skills, knowledge, and expertise and how, or if, your offering fills a need. Remember, consultants are problem solvers. What problems do organizations and individuals have that you can help them solve? More importantly, who will hire you to solve their problems?

Your potential clients will fall into two broad categories: businesses and individuals. Business clients look to consultants for help with:

- Accumulating capital for a business venture
- Launching a new product
- Entering a new market
- Expanding their share in an existing market
- Computerizing business processes
- Reorganizing the corporation
- Planning or updating employee compensation and benefits programs
- Implementing or upgrading computer systems
- Opening a new office, branch, or division

- Dealing with mergers and acquisitions
- Increasing productivity
- Reducing costs
- Improving quality control

Individuals tend to hire consultants for guidance about more personal issues, such as:

- Writing a résumé
- Finding a job
- Selecting a career
- Learning to use new software
- Learning foreign languages and gaining cultural insights
- Getting motivated
- Improving workplace skills
- Enjoying better relationships
- Feeling better about themselves
- Becoming healthier and more physically fit

If your area of expertise includes a niche or very specific skills, knowledge, or experience, you should consider promoting yourself as a specialist. Clients tend to prefer specialists because specialists can immediately step in, take over, and do the job alone, without supervision—quickly, correctly, and competently.

Consequently, specialists are almost always paid better and are in more demand than generalists. If you cannot identify a specialty right now, you have time to make that determination later. In many cases, consultants seem to drift toward a specialty by accident or circumstance rather than by deliberately choosing it.

PROVIDING SERVICES

Finally, in defining your marketable skills, experience, and knowledge, give some thought to how you will provide services. Consulting services can be grouped into five categories: advisory services, implementation services, training and development, publishing and product development, and contract and temporary consulting.

In a nutshell, these categories describe the various capacities or ways in which you can offer your marketable skills, knowledge, and experience. A more detailed description of each of the consulting services categories is below.

Advisory services. Most consultants act as advisors. They give recommendations and suggestions, but they don't implement their ideas, and they aren't the ones who decide which recommendations will be put into action.

Implementation services. Some consultants implement the solutions they (or others) come up with. An accountant, for example, not only shows you ways to get a tax refund, but also completes your return. A computer consultant, in addition to recommending a computing solution, may assemble the components, install and integrate them at the customer's site, do the custom programming, train the client to use the system, and even provide ongoing maintenance and support.

Training and development. Many consultants specialize in training the employees of client organizations in various job-related skills. About half of the nation's annual training budget goes toward basic and "soft" skills (business writing, customer service, teamwork, leadership, management, time management), while the other half is spent training employees in technical and "hard" skills (local area network troubleshooting, Microsoft Office, sales forecasting, compensation management, regulatory compliance).

Publishing and product development. The late consultant Howard Shenson said, "Publishing is every consultant's second job." Much of the information disseminated through consulting can be packaged and sold as "information products," including books, audios, workbooks, software, forms, checklists, phone support lines, Internet support, newsletters, and reference guides. Thus, there is an opportunity for almost every consultant to package part of his or her expertise as information products.

Contract and temporary consulting. Contractors and temps usually operate somewhat differently than a traditional independent consultant. The contract or temp typically works full-time on the client's premises, devoting all or most of their week to that client for as long as they are on the assignment. They perform a variety of tasks in addition to just giving advice, often working for the duration of the project as part of a team comprised of both consultants and staff workers.

Make the Most of Your Age Advantages

As a 50+ consultant, you should take into consideration how and if your age will impact your ability to provide consulting services in any or all of the categories listed above. In other words, is the particular service capacity "age appropriate?" Age appropriateness refers to the physical demands, schedule flexibility, and level of social interaction in the context of your own personal circumstance.

As a general matter, what makes consulting such an ideal profession for the older crowd is that the type and amount of work you do is totally up to you. So, when considering how you will be providing your services, you need to think carefully about the physical, mental, and time constraints involved. For example, you can probably safely assume that if your consulting services are limited to an advisory role or to publishing and product development, you will have few if any age-related challenges. A lot of your work can be done from your home, and travel will be limited.

Similarly, contract and temp consulting can be advantageous for older consultants because your services are clearly time-limited, giving you the opportunity to schedule and take care of matters related to your own health needs or caring for older parents.

Implementation consulting, on the other hand, depending upon what type of service you are actually offering, may be more physically challenging and consume more of your precious time. For example, if your computer systems consulting services are to include an implementation component, are you able to meet and sustain the physical challenges of actually installing the hardware associated with the computer system you have developed?

The bottom line is that being able to identify the requirements of each type of consulting category will help you better identify how you want to conduct your consulting business, how you want to promote it, and which potential clients will likely be most interested in what you have to offer.

Straight Talk from Bob

In 1979, my first job out of college was with Westinghouse, working as a junior member of the marketing communications department. My salary was an eye-popping $74 a day—about $9.25 an hour.

Right away, an interesting project came up, and I asked my boss to put me on it.

He thought I was too inexperienced. Instead, he called in a high-priced consultant. The guy did, in my opinion, an extremely mediocre job. Yet amazingly, the product manager seemed reasonably satisfied.

The job took the consultant three days. And, at $1,000 a day—almost 14 times more per day than the company was paying me—he billed the company $3,000.

To this day, I believe I could have done as good a job or better than the consultant did. Even if the job had taken me four days, it would have cost my company only $296 instead of $3,000.

"Hey, how long has this racket been going on?" I asked myself.

If a company was willing to pay an outsider more than 10 times what I was earning for essentially the same work, I reasoned I could make more money as an outside consultant than as an employee.

Not long after that, I quit the corporate world for good and I hung out my shingle as an independent consultant and copywriter.

I've never looked back.

4

Home-Based Business Opportunity #3: Coaching

Closely related to consulting is coaching. Consulting helps clients solve specific problems, while coaching gives clients ongoing guidance and motivation to achieve broad goals.

In the 1960s, advertising executive and satirist Stan Freberg wrote a song called "Betsy Ross and the Flag: Everybody Wants to Be an Art Director." In the 21st century, the title of the song could be "Everybody Wants to Be a Coach." Coaching, along with Internet marketing, is one of the hottest business opportunities today. Could you make a living as a coach?

By the time you are 50, you've spent years making a living through one or more venues in life. Now you would be happy to teach others how to do the same thing—and pay your bills while doing it. Being an independent coach may very well be one of the most rewarding careers you can get into, and it is perfectly suited as a home-based business. Plus, your years of experience and wisdom could make you quite attractive for those 30-something, would-be entrepreneurs out there who are "only now" realizing they could use some help figuring all this out.

Is This for Me?

Before you hang a whistle around your neck and call yourself a coach, make sure you've had some solid, successful experience in whatever area you plan to specialize in. You can only be a successful coach if you've got the background—if you've experienced the ups and downs in that niche and can show others how you handled difficult situations or overcame roadblocks. It is good if you have already taught classes or guest lectured in the area in which you would like to coach. If so, you'll certainly know if you have the talent to relate and successfully impart to others what you know that they need to know.

How would you go about building your coaching business? Your first step will be to decide which of the lessons you have learned in your life could be valuable to others. Sit down and make a list of what you have done in your life so far. From that list, determine what you feel you are quite good at and then narrow that list down further to the areas you would like to coach others in.

Your next step is to outline how you would go about building this kind of business and what you will need to practice the type of coaching you want to offer. There are two broad areas of coaching: One is physical coaching and the other is motivational coaching—working with a client to change thinking patterns rather than physical skills.

Needless to say, if you are a football (physical) coach, you will need a playing field and a gym, along with a team. But as a home-based motivational coach, you might be able to provide your services over the phone or by e-mail. So, you see how you could take a coaching career two different directions—physical or motivational—or combine it into one coaching package.

Consulting vs. Coaching

At this point, you might ask "What is the difference between consulting and coaching?" Let's compare a business coach to a business consultant.

A business consultant talks with a client, either by phone or in a personal visit to the client's place of business, usually about a particular action the business wants to take. For instance, a marketing consultant helping to create a particular sales campaign would ask how customer data is being gathered and analyzed and what strategies are used for approaching customers. The sales campaign would be analyzed and the consultant would offer suggestions about materials and copy to be sent out. The business consultant would help develop new strategies and guidelines for the client, based on weaknesses that already exist in the overall program. A consultant focuses on fixing *processes*.

In contrast, a business coach would concentrate more on the *client* and less on the processes, working to change how a client might see himself in his business. Business coaches focus more on motivational strategies, helping clients rethink their participation in the business and providing guidance toward more positive and productive thinking. Coaching is more about working with clients to change their thinking and develop natural talents that enhance not only themselves, but their business, as well.

HOW BOB DOES IT

If you pay attention to e-mails you get from information marketers, you notice that, in addition to selling you their content, they are also giving a lot of their content away. As a business coach, you should consider doing the same. Why?

Because if all you are doing is selling, your prospects will stop reading your e-mails or letters or listening to your presentations. But if you offer a combination of both free and paid content, they will stay interested and keep reading or listening. They will also appreciate the free stuff you give them and pay back your generosity by ordering more from you.

What can you give away for free? Well, links that let your readers watch a free video online. Or listen to an audio mp3 file. Or receive invitations to attend free webinars, or to receive free special reports and e-books.

How do you know what content to give away versus what content you charge for? My rule of thumb, given to me by Internet marketing consultant Wendy Montes de Oca, is this:

Your free content tells your readers what to do. Your paid content tells them how to do it.

For example, in an e-mail newsletter, I have revealed the five best ways to promote yourself as a freelance copywriter and explained what the five methods are. But in the limited space of an e-mail, I could not possibly explain how to do each.

However, I do sell information products that teach how to perform each method in great detail. And, I offer these to my readers at a reasonable price.

Consider how you could adapt that technique to your coaching business.

Who Hires a Coach?

To gauge whether you would like to be a coach, you should first understand who your potential clients would be. Who hires a coach? Anyone who needs extra help to pull something together.

Sometimes people might find themselves at a loss as to how to proceed in a new business. Maybe they want to give presentations to large audiences or sell a product or service but are fearful of public speaking. Or, maybe they don't believe they are good at sales. So they look for someone who has a successful history of speaking in front of large audiences or running effective sales campaigns to coach them. Coaches can offer a number of techniques that will allow people to move past their fears of failure and become immersed in the presentations they want to give or to create the campaigns they want to carry out. Most of this can be taught in one-on-one situations over several coaching sessions.

One coaching/consulting firm, Passion for Business, lists on its website (www.passionforbusiness.com) some of the types of clients the company has assisted through its coaching or consulting services, or, in some cases, a combination of the two:

- Accountant
- Adult education school owner
- Alternative medicine healer
- Animal trainer
- Attorney
- Author
- Business consultant
- Calligrapher
- Career counselor
- Caterer
- Chiropractor
- Clergy coach
- Copywriter
- Dance studio owner

- Divorce mediator
- Employment agency owner
- Event planner
- Financial advisor/planner
- Fitness center designer
- Graphic designer
- Holistic healer
- House painter and restorer
- Instructional designer/trainer
- Interior decorator
- Jewelry designer
- Life coach
- Marketing consultant
- Meeting planner
- Motivational speaker
- Multi-level marketer
- Online distance-learning school owner
- Outplacement facilitator
- Organizational development consultant
- Personal chef
- Photographer
- Professional organizer
- Professional speaker
- Psychotherapist
- Real estate agent/broker
- Real estate investor
- Retail store owner
- Small business coach

- Venture capital consultant
- Virtual assistant
- Wedding planner
- Yoga and Pilates instructor

To get an idea about how you might set up a coaching business, take a look at the way Passion For Business operates, which includes a variety of phone-based coaching programs. One, the comprehensive 90-day strategy and planning program, is offered for about $1,400 and includes nine 45-minute phone consultations over 90 days. Also, part of the program consists of unlimited short consulting e-mails and access to a client-only website that is chock-full of related resources.

A less comprehensive package is offered for about $500 and includes three 45-minute phone consultations, unlimited short consulting e-mails, and access to the client-only website. Or, the company will provide individual coaching for about $225 per hour.

What Could I Coach?

There are many avenues you could explore if you want to be a coach, either physical, motivational, or both. Consider all the skills you have learned in a lifetime of work and through your hobbies and leisure activities to see if there are some you could pass along as a coach.

For example, if you spent years as a professional ballerina with several ballet companies and performed many leading roles, you could become a private coach to aspiring ballerinas. You might be lucky enough to have a large house with one big room that could be converted into a dance studio where you could work with your clients. Or, you could rent a studio from a dance school during hours when there are no classes or rehearsals.

Voice coaches are often in high demand, especially for clients new to the speech and presentation circuits. If you have background in this area, you can work with a client on speech patterns and breathing techniques. No one wants to listen to a speaker for more than 10 minutes if that speaker's voice is monotone and boring.

> **Word to the Wise**
>
> Be aware that anytime you bring people to your home, you should have insurance to cover yourself in case of any accident on your property. You can also have your clients sign release forms if insurance is too expensive for the type of business coaching you are conducting. Check with a lawyer. Also, be aware of neighborhood zoning issues that might prevent you from bringing people to your home in a business capacity.

Maybe your way of relaxing from your stressful job for the past few decades has been to head to the shooting range or enter shooting competitions. You could turn that hobby into a coaching role. If you haven't already, take the programs offered by the National Rifle Association (NRA), which certifies you in pistol, rifle, shotgun, and home protection. Once you go through the program, you will most likely start out working with other coaches in group situations, possibly as part of community service with a firearms club.

When you have enough experience training others in this type of setting, you can start your own coaching service. Take advantage of local and regional shooting competitions, which teach you to perform under stress and will be a great place to publicize your skills and your business. Normally, private coaching fees can run from $50 to $100 per hour, depending on whether you are working with a new client who has never shot before or someone who already shoots pistols but wants to learn how to handle a shotgun.

Coaching Life Skills

Motivational coaching, along with life coaching, can cover many areas of life, including the two previous examples of ballet and firearms coaching. Instead of teaching students how to perform the physical moves needed to succeed at a difficult ballet variation or timed shooting competition, you could teach what mental adjustments could help a client be successful.

For example, dancer may fear having to make a series of difficult turns during a variation. A motivational coach can help the dancer mentally picture a successful completion of these turns ahead of time, lessening the fears of those turns. The pressure of having many people watching during a competition can be intimidating and stressful to shooters. A coach could train the shooter to forget the audience and improve concentration and focus.

Being a motivational and life coach can be very rewarding when you see your clients overcoming personal hang-ups and pushing forward to accomplish what they want to do. Motivational coaches can help people in any number of professions or lifestyles. A mom who is home all day with young kids may need a life coach to help her accomplish more at home and take control of her lifestyle. The coach goes into the home, watches what goes on there for a day or two, and then offers the mom some ideas about how she can more effectively accomplish what she needs to do in a way that is more fulfilling to her. This type of coaching is ideal for women who have successfully navigated similar passages in their lives and have developed strategies that could be helpful to others.

Connecting Remotely

Coaching doesn't always have to be done in person. Many lessons can be offered through CD or video programs. For instance, Dr. Joe Vitale, one of several contributors to the best-selling movie "The Secret," has developed a CD program called "The Secret to Attracting Money." The program is marketed to anyone interested in how to become wealthy, changing mind sets, persuasion techniques, and the law of attraction. This program is an example of providing coaching on a remote basis.

Even if you are not as famous as Dr. Vitale, you can produce a similar program; make the program more interactive through your website and include personal coaching phone calls as part of the package. Or, you can offer a monthly coaching program for a small fee for each month. Get enough folks to sign up for the program, and then stretch it out over 12 to 24 months, and you would be bringing in a very nice income!

The most important aspect to remember about coaching is that you must always show your client how to take action. Coaching is not solely about changing the way your clients thinks … it's also about teaching them how to take action along with those changes in thought processes. Coaching a client to get past the nonaction (fear of failure) point can go a long way to providing a successful outcome for a client. The foundation must be laid first … and then the structure built, piece by piece.

Researching Before Coaching

If you think coaching might be right for you, and you have determined a niche you would love to work in, it's time to start market research. If you are going to be a localized coach, search for everyone who does this type of coaching in your area. Find out how they set up their programs and ask how much they charge. What you learn will give you a pretty good basis for building your own program, determining what you can offer, especially if it's new and interesting, and then getting to the business of marketing.

Once you have completed this step of your homework, find out who would be interested in a program such as the one you are going to offer. Should you place ads in local publications or should the coverage be more national? Do you have a website for your business? If not, get one set up before you do any advertising whatsoever! Your future customers need to know where they can get more information and how they can contact you.

You can find more general advice about creating marketing and advertising campaigns, as well as a list of resources, later in this book. But if you are offering coaching services, remember that you are actually selling yourself—not a product off the shelf. So, your advertising and marketing materials need to provide potential customers with at least a glimpse of you and give them reasons to trust you.

If you are not a writer and don't feel you can create the materials needed for an effective sales campaign, hire a copywriter who has some background in your niche. If necessary, hire a photographer who can take pictures of you in action. Your customers want to know what you look like, which will give them a first impression of who they are dealing with. Hint: Now is the time to dress up in business clothes, suit or nice jacket, and shirt. A professional appearance will inspire more confidence in your potential customers. Hide the tattoos and biker leathers for another photo session … unless you are providing coaching lessons about how to drive a motorcycle in bad weather. It's all about your market and attracting it to you!

Straight Talk from Bob

Although I think coaching is a great business for people who like to give guidance and advice, I have never been one of those people and so have never offered coaching services. But a recent event prompts me to offer some motivational, life skills advice that could be useful no matter what kind of business you choose to set up.

I have often been a complainer and even a whiner, but when Hurricane Sandy barreled into my home state of New Jersey in 2012, I learned that most of what I had been complaining about was really petty.

The storm destroyed many homes in the state. Others were so damaged the residents had to move to shelters. Power was out for millions of people for days or weeks.

At my house, we felt we dodged a bullet. During the height of the storm, we lost power, huge branches came down in our tree-filled yard, and screen windows flew off the house. A tall, skinny tree on the front lawn bent like a blade of grass in the wind, and we were certain it would hit the house. Again, we were lucky.

For days and weeks after the storm, residents had to deal with gasoline rationing. People in lines at gas stations easily faced two- to three-hour waits. Fortunately, since I worked at home, I didn't have to drive to work or go anywhere else.

Hurricane Sandy reminded me in a real way that we shouldn't sweat the small stuff, because there are really bad things that can happen to people—things that most of us are lucky enough to dodge—but some can't.

I don't want to minimize the very real problems that can come up when you are trying to set up a new business. They can be painful and frustrating.

But my new attitude is this: Any day you wake up in good health with a roof over your head and food to eat is a good day.

This attitude of gratitude has brought me some peace and contentment. I hope it can do the same for you.

5

Home-Based Business Opportunity #4: eBay

With low start-up costs and a user-friendly operation, selling on eBay can be a simple and profitable way to establish and run a home business.

Maybe you just want to clear up some space in your house and would like to be able to bring in some extra cash in the process. By the time you pass your 50th birthday, your closets, shelves, garages, and every other nook and cranny may be filled to overflowing. You would love to get rid of some of this stuff, but the idea of tossing perfectly good _____ (fill in the blank) in the trash appalls you. So, why not set up an eBay account? If you can bring in a few bucks for your items, you will feel a lot less ambivalent about parting with some long-held possessions.

Or, maybe you would prefer to use eBay to build a full-fledged, home-based business. You know where you can find last year's models of _____ (fill in the blank) for a very good price. You would like to find a place to sell these models, but definitely don't want to open a storefront or go door-to-door; eBay may be just the business for you.

Is This for Me?

"Learn how to sell in just 4 simple steps: list, sell, ship, and get paid." That's what eBay says on its website. Sounds easy enough, but then you notice that there's a 23-page "Get Started" guide to download and dozens of links to more pages with tips and instructions, links to videos and tutorials, and even links to eBay University, where you find more links to dozens of classes on a variety of ways you can sell on eBay. It's dawning on you that mastering those four simple steps may not be quite so simple. In its early days, eBay was like a giant, digital garage sale. Now, it's more like a giant, digital, fiercely competitive retail center.

Who can succeed in that environment? People who understand and thrive in sales and marketing, that's who. If you're over 50 and have spent your career in sales or retail marketing, selling on eBay might be the perfect home-based business for you. To succeed in the new eBay environment, you need to understand how to price and market merchandise and how to provide great customer service. Many sellers on eBay still think it's a giant garage sale and have no idea how to display or advertise or price their merchandise to provide themselves a profit. You've been honing those skills for decades while selling someone else's merchandise under someone else's rules. Now, you can take your knowledge and experience online and set up your own shop on eBay with little overhead and no one looking over your shoulder or dictating your every move.

But before you jump in with both feet, you also need to understand that to be successful on eBay, you will need to have a better-than-average grasp of computers, Internet transactions, and digital technology. Let's face it—many people over 50 are not all that comfortable with computers and the new digital landscape. So, before you grab for the eBay ring, honestly consider your computer skills. You will need to understand digital terms and vocabulary; be comfortable establishing eBay and PayPal accounts and individual pages and settings within those accounts; remember a boatload of passwords and usernames; navigate various menus and commands that frequently change when a program or process is updated; take digital photos of merchandise; upload text and pictures; arrange for product shipping; and answer customer queries by e-mail. If you know you're not really up for these challenges, think about hiring someone to help with the technical stuff.

What Is eBay?

It all started with trading Pez dispensers online—or so the story goes. In reality, eBay's first transaction was even more unusual: a broken laser pointer that sold for $14.83. Pierre Omidyar was surprised by the interest in a "broken" laser pointer, and the eBay phenomenon began.

The online auction service was originally called AuctionWeb. The first auction took place on Labor Day 1995, and it was only a matter of weeks before a myriad of buyers and sellers discovered the site. Becoming a word-of-mouth phenomenon, the company grew rapidly. AuctionWeb was incorporated in 1996; the name was changed to eBay in 1997; and the company went public in 1998.

What Pierre Omidyar began as a hobby in 1995 has grown into a multi-billion dollar business with operations localized in more than thirty countries.

How eBay Works

eBay is an online auction site with all the excitement of a real, live auction. You bid. You hold your breath while someone outbids you. You bid again. You wait for your opponent's next move. For the seller, it is equally exciting because you create a pricing strategy, put a product up for bid, and watch the action. Or, you can offer items on a "Buy It Now" basis so that customers can skip the bidding. Easily addictive, buying and selling on eBay can be both fun and profitable.

The requirements are simple. Registration and setup take a matter of minutes. No special tools or software are required, and there is a wealth of information online to help you figure out how to get started. The "Seller Information Center" offers information and tutorials about dozens of aspects of selling on eBay, and you can find books, websites, adult-school classes, and online courses all dedicated to teaching you how to make money through eBay.

eBay makes money in several ways: through listing transaction fees, special features, selling transaction fees, and advertising. You can choose from a variety of ways to pay eBay for listing on its site, from simple nonrefundable fees to percentages of sales price, and may also choose to pay for enhanced listings or services. The more you understand the various fee structures, the better you will be able to determine which ones will be the most beneficial to you. These fees and structures change fairly regularly, so make sure you study the very latest information that is available on the eBay site. It is important to understand the fees and know all of your true costs (including time spent) so that you can price your items appropriately and make money on every transaction.

How Selling Through eBay Can Be Profitable

eBay is the best-known online auction site and the one many people turn to first when they are looking for something unusual or hoping to buy something without paying full retail prices. Everyone loves a bargain, and eBay is the perfect place to find one online. The enthusiasm and sense of community on eBay can encourage buyers to compete with other buyers to get what they want in an auction setting; sometimes that excitement drives up prices, creating a buying frenzy.

If you are a seller who is highly rated on eBay and you market your products well, tremendous opportunity awaits you. With more than 200 million users, the audience is huge. It's just a matter of placing your products in the right section (categories and subcategories); using effective titles, descriptions and pictures to prominently display your products online; and having an effective pricing strategy.

While the process is easy, there is one step that you don't want to forget—research. Before you buy or sell a product, do some research online, both outside of eBay to learn more about the product, and by looking at the completed listings on eBay. These listings will show you similar items that have been listed on eBay in the past couple of weeks, whether they sold or not. If the item did sell, what price did it generally bring in? How did the successful seller market the item and what shipping practices were offered? This information will give you an idea of what you can typically buy or sell in a particular price range and also give you an idea of which techniques sell, including effective pictures, pricing strategies, descriptions, keywords, and appropriate categories.

Researching and understanding what the competition is offering, which auctions have been successful, and the nuts and bolts of how the product was marketed gives you an edge.

What Sells Well on eBay

Everything imaginable from the obscure to the ordinary finds its way to eBay. The following categories of items typically sell successfully on eBay:

- Antiques
- Art
- Books
- Business and industrial supplies
- Clothing, shoes, and accessories
- Coins
- Collectibles

- Computer products and networking services
- Consumer electronics
- Dolls and bears
- DVDs
- Health and beauty products
- Home goods
- Jewelry
- Music
- Musical instruments
- Cameras, camcorders
- Pottery and glass
- Sporting goods/fan memorabilia
- Sports cards
- Stamps
- Tickets
- Toys and hobbies
- Video games

WHO SELLS ON EBAY

A wide variety of businesses and proprietors are successful on eBay. Many people make eBay their primary income source, while others dabble here and there and use their eBay profits as extra spending money. Listed below are some types of people who find eBay a natural home for their home business:

SECOND-HAND RESELLER. This is your classic eBay seller. Individuals who have extra things in their garage, attic, or basement that they want to sell often choose eBay as the best way to recycle for a profit.

COLLECTOR/TRADER. Consistent with the founding idea of the site, many collectors of a wide variety of items developed a successful home-based business trading on eBay. The very foundation of eBay's culture and practices make this type of business quite viable for those individuals who have the time and interest to pursue it.

Bulk reseller. Many people have established successful eBay businesses by buying in bulk at a low price and then selling on eBay at a higher price. To make this a profitable business, the eBay seller needs to be aware of his/her true costs, including time spent both selling goods and acquiring goods to sell. With high-volume sales and a good source for merchandise, this can be a very successful business. For example, someone may buy T-shirts with trendy designs in bulk and then resell them on eBay for a profit.

Artists/designers/craftspeople. eBay is an excellent option for artists or designers to display and sell their creations. Whether you have jewelry, sketches, handmade toys, or decorations, eBay lets creative individuals test and then establish a business selling their unique designs or artwork.

General retailer. This eBay entrepreneur buys wholesale and sells retail—similar to a traditional store, but usually without the overhead of a brick-and-mortar location or the need for regular operating hours. This is also an opportunity for multilevel marketers to sell extra product inventory online.

In addition to professional general retailers, many people over 50 fall into one or more of these categories. It's not unusual for people at this age to suddenly acquire several households full of belongings as aging relatives die or leave their homes. Or, maybe they decide to finally part with a comic book or baseball card collection or take up a hobby such as painting or woodworking and need a place to peddle their wares. Perhaps a career of buying and selling for an employer has taught them how to find a good deal and now they want to make deals on their own. All of these people can find eBay the perfect venue for turning a profit.

Getting Started

To sell on eBay, go to ebay.com and register as a user and then set up a seller's account. Follow the detailed instructions on the site to complete the process; you will have to provide the usual types of contact information, plus some personal details so that eBay can verify your identity and intentions. You will also have to select how you want to pay for seller fees and sign up for a PayPal account, although there is no charge until you begin selling.

You can also register your eBay account as a business, which allows you to add a business name to your account. If you are specializing in a particular area (for example, selling handmade doorstops), it adds credibility if you are set up as a business and have a name that reflects your niche market. You can select the name that is most appropriate for the items you are selling, or eBay will recommend a name.

In order to create and protect a successful business selling (and/or buying) on eBay, there are a few things you will want to have:

- Personal computer with Internet access
- Computer virus protection
- PayPal account
- Digital camera
- Fabric or different-colored sheets to use as a backdrop to display your items in photos

Hanging Out Your "For Sale" Sign

When you are ready to offer an item for sale on eBay, you can choose to sell through the online auction, where potential customers bid for an object that is sold to the highest bidder, or, if certain conditions are met, you can offer your product for a fixed price.

Because millions of items are listed on eBay at any one time, you will have to be sure that potential customers see your product. So, you must choose carefully how you list, describe, and price your product. Do your research; view the completed listings to see how similar products have been sold. What category were they listed in? What description of the item was given? How did the seller set the starting bid, and what was the ultimate selling price? Don't rush through these steps just in order to see your own product online.

Word to the Wise

You can find much information about how to sell on eBay. Look for books and websites dedicated to the topic. Seek out online courses or classes offered in your community. Read the tips that successful sellers have posted in blogs or newsletters. Dig through the tips and history offered on the eBay site. The more you know about the process and the more you understand about what sells at what price, the more successful you will be.

Pay particular attention to how you set your starting price and whether you want to include a reserve price. The starting price is where bidding will begin, and it is usually recommended that you start low to generate interest and enthusiasm. Posting a reserve price—the minimum amount at which you will sell the item—is optional. You also need to give some thought to how long your auction will last and what dates it will begin and end.

Listings with photos are most likely to generate interest. Even when you are selling something like event tickets, photos help potential buyers feel more secure that they are bidding on something they want to receive. Always be sure that your listings explain your shipping policies and fees, your return policies, and what forms of payment you will accept.

Show 'em What You Got

If you're going to make money selling on eBay, you really need to include pictures. Since a buyer is not able to see and touch your product, they want to see a vivid picture of what they are buying online. There are ways to get a version of your picture on eBay even without a digital camera, but a digital camera will make it easier for you. There are a variety of options you can choose when it comes to including pictures for the items you are selling: Read the fine print for all products and services so that you understand what is being offered and how much it will cost you. Look carefully at your listing when it is posted and see if it looks like you expected.

Background and lighting are important when you are taking photos of your merchandise. If you are displaying a relatively small product (e.g. jewelry), using a plain white cloth or sheet as a backdrop allows the potential buyer to focus on the product without distraction. Another option is to place your item on inexpensive fabric swatches that show off your product in the best light. Make sure that you get close enough to your product so that there is not too much empty space, which will make it look small.

After you have some good pictures of your products, follow the instructions on eBay's website for how to upload the photos with your listing.

Seller Beware

More than 99 percent of transactions on eBay go as planned, and most people you will do business with are honest. However, there are a few things to watch out for, including "phishing," a type of online fraud.

When someone sends you an e-mail that looks like it is from an authentic source, such as your bank or eBay, and informs you there is a problem with your account, and asks you to log into the site and provide your user name and password so they can repair the account, they are "phishing" for information. The e-mail will not take you to the site you expect, but will send you to a phony web page. You should be wary of e-mails from either PayPal or eBay that take you to a site and ask you to fill in your name and password. The e-mail and website may look like the real thing, but they are probably frauds.

How do you protect yourself? First, know that neither eBay nor PayPal will ever send you an e-mail telling you to follow a link and then sign in after you have become a member. So, you should never click on a link from an e-mail that looks like it is from eBay or PayPal. If you need to check something out, you can go to their websites and sign in without using the link. As another precaution, use the best anti-virus and anti-phishing protection that is suitable for your computer and software.

It is also a good idea to have different user names and passwords for eBay and PayPal. If hackers or scammers do somehow manage to get your information at one site, you don't want them to be able to get into both accounts at the same time.

You should also take steps to protect yourself from buyer fraud, such as buyers claiming they didn't receive the merchandise they paid for or using a stolen credit card to make a purchase. Use delivery services that provide tracking information and proof of receipt, and use PayPal or a similar service that offer you some protection from fraud.

One of the most useful and popular features on eBay is the ability to provide feedback if a buyer or seller does not deliver as promised. The feedback on potential buyers' profile pages can give you a clue about whether you should trust them to deliver their payment as expected.

Straight Talk from Bob

Recently, dozens of my websites were hacked at one time. From that experience, I learned that worries about hacking reaching epidemic proportions are not exaggerated.

I discovered that as of late 2012, the U.S. Congress and the executive branch are under cyber attack an incredible 1.8 billion times a month. The cyber-security market is expected to reach $21 billion by 2015. Half of 240 web developers surveyed by the research firm Forrester had suffered at least one security breach in the previous 18 months.

If you are relying on income from an eBay business, you MUST take computer security very seriously. I am no expert in computer security, but here are a few tips for safeguarding your website and hard drive, provided by some of my readers and experts:

- If you have multiple websites, host them on different servers and hosting services. That way, if one server is infected with a virus, not all your sites go down.
- Linux servers of any kind are less vulnerable to hacking than Windows servers.
- Install a firewall to prevent worms, Trojan viruses, and spyware from infecting your system.
- When you're not using your computer, turn it off. Hackers can't get into a computer that is shut down.
- Change all your passwords periodically.
- Schedule regular backups of your website code and databases, so you can restore the site if it is hacked.
- Immediately alert your webmaster that you've been hacked and task him or her with fixing the situation … and ask him why he allowed it to happen in the first place.
- My site was hacked through an old WordPress installation or WordPress plug-in. Our webmaster modified security scripts to prohibit WordPress or its plug-ins from making changes to any files in the sites.

- Research plug-ins before you download them. See if there are any reported security breaches. Hackers use plug-ins as "back doors" into your systems.
- If you are using old versions of any software, upgrade to the current versions.
- Have your webmaster check your HTML source code for hidden links that may have been inserted by hackers.
- Don't open e-mail attachments from people you don't know. Don't run or download programs from unfamiliar sources.
- Have your webmaster disable unused ActiveX and JavaScript content, which hackers can use to hack into your programs.
- Use a strong open-source content management system (CMS) instead of a straight HTML CMS, which is vulnerable to hackers.
- Instruct your webmaster to look for and eliminate badly programmed scripts, as any of them found by hackers can allow root access to your machine.
- Test your password at www.PasswordMeter.com. You should score 80 percent or higher to qualify as a strong password. And be sure to use different passwords in different places.
- Encrypt passwords you store on your computer. Don't just store them in a Word document or spreadsheet, where any virus you catch can find the file.
- Have your web hosting company ban IP addresses from people trying to access websites to hack them.

6

Home-Based Business Opportunity #5: Internet Marketing

Selling on the Internet is approaching a trillion-dollar market. According to J. P. Morgan, global e-commerce revenues will hit $963 billion by 2013. Even a microscopic market share of the e-commerce marketplace can make an entrepreneur rich beyond the dreams of avarice.

Selling products from your own websites is a bit more complicated than selling from eBay, but it offers even greater profit potential. I started my first Internet marketing business when I was 48. Today, I am 54, and my Internet business averages $1,000 a day in passive income, with me "working" on the business only an hour a day.

It wasn't always that way. Once you have built up your Internet business, it's true that you can make a lot of money with little effort. However, starting up an Internet marketing business takes a lot of work up front and is anything but the "get rich quick" scheme that so many online promoters promise it will be.

Is This for Me?

The primary thing you need to succeed in Internet marketing is specialized knowledge that other people will pay to obtain. That knowledge can be about almost anything: training dogs, designing dresses, improving your golf game, investing in bonds, growing medicinal herbs—you get the idea. If you're over 50, you are very likely to have some information and wisdom that you would be willing to share for a price. Maybe it's knowledge you learned from decades in a particular industry or business; maybe it's something you learned while dealing with a difficult life situation or from years pursuing a particular hobby.

Sharing your knowledge through Internet marketing can be very lucrative. But if you're considering this type of business, you need to know that Internet marketing is driven largely by words. You must be able to incorporate keywords into your marketing, Google Adwords advertisements, web pages, online newsletters, e-mails, and more. You will either need to have good writing skills, be willing to develop those skills, or be ready to outsource the writing to professional writers. (You can look for affordable writing help at www.elance.com.)

You also will need to have some understanding of how to set up websites and how to use keywords and search-engine optimization to make sure that potential clients can find your material. If you don't have intimate knowledge of such issues, you can hire professional website developers and programmers (www.elance.com is, again, just one of many spots where you can look for such help).

A Lucrative Client

When you develop skill in writing as I have, one lucrative avenue is, as we've already discussed, to freelance. For many decades, I've earned a six-figure income writing ads, sales letters, and other marketing materials for both local and national clients.

But within the past few years, I've written for a client whose work is more lucrative for me than even my biggest Fortune 500 accounts. That client is CTC Publishing, a tiny, one-person business selling "information products"—e-books, audio albums, DVDs, and teleseminars—over the Internet.

And the reason it's so lucrative for me is that CTC Publishing is me. For about six years, I've made a handsome spare-time income—thousands of extra dollars a week in sales—writing and selling my own "how-to" information products (mostly about writing, freelancing, and marketing) online. In this chapter, I want to show you how to do the same.

I'm so enthusiastic about Internet marketing that I tell every writer I meet that marketing your own information products online should be every writer's second business. And, maybe it should be yours, too, whether you like to write or not. You don't have to be a writer to earn six figures online. Information products aren't the only things you can sell online, although they require the least storage space and start-up capital.

You can sell merchandise on the Internet and even professional and trade services, such as consulting, coaching, carpentry, and construction. But for many beginners, selling information products online is the way to go. You own the exclusive rights to information products you create, and your product is unique.

Writing for traditional clients, as lucrative as it can be, is—like just about every other type of freelance writing—extremely labor intensive. You get paid only when you work. Stop writing or stop pursuing assignments and your income drops to zero.

Collecting Passively

Internet marketing is different because it gives you passive income. You create an information product one time and then sell it forever, making money with each sale, with minimal additional labor involved. Orders come into my online shopping cart, often with no activity on my part, every day of the week, including weekends and holidays. (You will need a shopping cart to take orders online, and I recommend WebMarketingMagic.com.)

The profit margins for Internet marketing are astronomically higher than those in traditional book publishing. Example: I wrote a trade paperback for a major New York publishing house. On each sale, after paying my agent his commission, I made a total of 72 cents profit per book. When the 200-page paperback went out of print, the rights reverted to me.

I scanned the book, updated it, and republished it as a series of three e-books priced at $29 each. Thereafter, each time I sold the same content in e-book form online, I made $87 instead of 72 cents. Because an e-book is a downloadable PDF file, there is no printing cost, no inventory to store, and no shipping cost. Your profit margin is virtually 100 percent. Had I republished the book as a self-published trade paperback, my profit margin would have been 50 percent or less.

Transforming a Niche into an Empire

The first step to becoming a successful Internet information marketer is to pick a topic or niche. You must build your online information empire around a tightly focused subject area. All information products you write and sell must relate to this niche. You can't jump from cats to gardening to yoga. You must pick a core topic and build your online information empire around it. For instance, if your first information product is on setting up a saltwater aquarium, your second could be on marine fish illnesses and how to treat them.

How do you choose a publishing niche that is both fun and profitable? Start by asking yourself a few questions: What interests you? What do you know? What experiences do you have? What is your education? What do you enjoy writing about that others will pay to learn?

Before committing to a niche, make sure there is sufficient online interest in the topic. Here's how to do so: Go to www.WordTracker.com and type in the keywords that best describe your niche (e.g., "breeding tropical fish"). If the results show 10,000 or more monthly searches on those key words at Yahoo/Overture, that's a good indication that enough people are searching online for information on that topic to make it profitable.

Next, go to Google and search those same keywords. Are others selling information on that topic? If so, that's another good sign: It indicates that people will pay for information products on this subject. If no one is selling information products on that topic, but you find sites giving away information on it for free, that's a bad sign: It means people may want content but are not willing to pay for it.

Take note: This is essential. Once you select your subject niche, write and publish a monthly online newsletter on that topic. Don't charge for your e-newsletter (or e-zine). Give it away. By doing so, you build a list of subscribers who are (a) interested in the topic and (b) give you their e-mail address and permission to send e-mails to them. To see my monthly newsletter, click on www.bly.com/archive.

Create an interesting special report or short tip sheet on your topic. Offer it free as a bonus gift to people who subscribe to your e-zine. Create a web page where people can sign up for your e-newsletter and get your free bonus gift. This is known in Internet marketing as a "name squeeze page."

You can see my name squeeze page at www.bly.com/reports. Sign up for my newsletter and you get a library of marketing reports with a retail value of $116 absolutely free. By offering this valuable bribe, I convince nearly one out of every two people who visit my squeeze page to subscribe to my e-list. This is the primary vehicle through which I have built my list of 65,000 online subscribers.

How Bob Does It

When I put up my first website, experts told me I should have a lot of articles on the site for SEO (search-engine optimization) purposes. But writing good articles is a lot of work and would have taken a long time—and I wanted to get the website up ASAP.

Then I remembered that in the 1980s and 1990s, before I got online, I had written dozens of business articles on marketing topics for print publications. I didn't have the original Word files for most of these articles, but I knew that I had tear sheet copies of all my articles.

I had file cabinets in the basement, and the bottom drawer of one held tear sheets of all my articles. The only problem: Our elderly cat had peed into the open drawer, and all the articles were covered with a foul-smelling yellow powder that prevented them from being scanned. So, I made a clear photocopy of each original, handling them with tweezers and gloves, and then scanned those clean copies.

In speeches, I call this "the cat piss story."

The real lesson is not to keep your files away from the cat, but to protect your digital assets carefully. Content is gold on the Internet today, and there may just be a small fortune hidden on your hard drive.

Three Steps to Six Figures

You need only three things to make a six-figure income selling information products on the Internet: products to sell, people to sell your products to, and a way to get those people to buy.

The "people to sell your products to" are your e-newsletter subscribers, as well as traffic that comes to your website. Obviously, your online revenues will increase proportionally with the size of the e-list you build. So, adding new subscribers is a primary goal of all Internet marketers and a never-ending activity.

You also need information products to sell to your online subscribers. My line of information products includes e-books, DVDs, and audio files. As a writer, the quickest and easiest way to create information products is to repurpose content you have already created and own the rights to. If you do not own content, you can take content that is in the public domain—meaning it is not copyrighted—and sell it online. For more information on selling public domain information, visit: www.PublicDomainRichesOnline.com.

When you speak, allow the conference sponsor to record your presentation, as long as you get a copy of the master and retain the rights to do with the audio or video as you please. At the last writer's conference where I spoke, I gave two presentations. Both were videotaped. I turned the recording into a video product (two DVDs in a vinyl case) that I sell online for $100.

OK. You have people to sell to (your e-newsletter/e-zine subscribers) and information products to sell them (your writings and lectures repackaged as DVDs, CDs, and e-books; original content; or public domain content). All you need now is a way to sell those products online to the people who want them.

Word to the Wise

As an information marketer, make sure you retain the copyright to everything you create. Your article contracts should state that you are selling "first rights only," so once your articles are published, you can repackage them into special reports or e-books. Your book contracts should state that when the book goes out of print, rights revert to the author, so you can republish your out-of-print trade books as e-books.

Building on a Landing Page

In Internet marketing, the standard tool for selling information products online is the landing page. A landing page is a stand-alone website dedicated to the sale of a single product. That means if you have six products, you need to create six separate landing pages.

The landing page is basically a long-copy sales letter posted on a server. Each landing page should have its own domain. Pick domain names related to the product title that are easy to remember. For instance, for an information product I sell on building a large and profitable e-list, my domain name is www.BuildYourListFast.net (the .com, always preferable, was taken). Go to that web address and you can see a sample landing page.

You can reserve domain names at www.UltraCheapDomains.com, where you can also find almost immediately whether the domain name you want is available. For free advice on how to write and design effective landing pages, visit www.TheLandingPageGuru.com. You will also need to arrange hosting for your multiple landing pages; I use www.HostWithStanley.com.

Not everybody who visits your landing pages will buy the product being advertised. In fact, most won't. Landing page effectiveness is measured by conversion rate, which is the percentage of visitors who buy the product. A 5 percent conversion rate is quite respectable, but if you get a 5 percent conversion, it means 95 out of 100 visitors to the page are not buying the product. Add a pop-up window or other device to your landing pages to capture the e-mail addresses of non-buyers so you can add them to your e-list. All of my landing pages have a button that says "newsletter" in the upper right corner of the first screen. When you click it, you can subscribe to my free newsletter.

Once you create and post landing pages for each of your products, how do you let your online subscribers know about them? The easiest and most effective way is to send them e-mail messages. Each e-mail message talks about one product and has a link to the URL of that product's landing page.

Is this spam? No. Remember, all of your online subscribers have given you their e-mail address voluntarily, along with their permission for you to send e-mail. More importantly, if they like your online newsletter and find its contents valuable, they have become interested in reading what you write and will therefore be more inclined to get more information from you, even when you start charging for it.

Internet information marketing is like playing the piano: difficult and complex to master at the highest levels, but fairly easy to do on a basic level. Remember, all you need are three things: people to sell to (your e-newsletter subscribers), something to sell them (your information products), and a way to sell it to them (landing pages and e-mail marketing messages). With just those three things, and nothing more, you can earn a spare-time, six-figure income writing and selling simple information online—just like I do.

Straight Talk from Bob

Many of my newsletter subscribers tell me they are "almost ready" to get into Internet marketing as soon as they finish doing a little more research, a little more reading. Frequently, my advice to them is "stop reading about it and stop talking about it and actually start doing it."

I'm not saying you shouldn't learn something about Internet marketing before you start. I am saying you do not need to learn *everything* about Internet marketing before you start.

It's simply Michael Masterson's success principle of "Ready, Fire, Aim" in action. And, it's especially true in Internet marketing. There is an oppressive mountain of boot camps ... courses ... seminars ... workbooks ... coaching programs ... DVDs ... websites ... audio CDs ... e-books ... reports ... and other "how to get rich quick on the Internet" material out there. (I sell some of it myself.)

Aspiring Internet marketers quite sensibly buy and study this material in preparation for the day when they start their own fledgling Internet marketing business. Unfortunately, for the vast majority, that day never comes. They get so caught up in reading and talking about Internet marketing, that they forget to actually do Internet marketing. And so they never graduate beyond the student phase and move into the real world.

The problem with this, of course, is that their knowledge remains theoretical and never becomes applied knowledge ... and they never make a dime from it.

To be sure, many people really enjoy reading how-to business books and studying marketing. If you're in that group, and all you want is a pleasant, intellectually stimulating hobby to pass the time, well, nothing wrong with that. Lots of people read and study for nothing other than the pleasure of learning.

But I'm guessing you want something more from studying Internet marketing than just entertainment. Specifically, you want to start and build a home-based Internet marketing business—and by doing so earn thousands of dollars a year in extra income.

So, when is the best time to start your new Internet marketing business? Quite simply, it's today. And here's how.

First, decide to work on your new business venture at least five days a week, at least an hour a day.

Second, make a list of 10 things you need to do to get the business off the ground.

When your hour to work on your business arrives, immediately start working on item number one on your top 10 things to-do list. Spend all your business start-up time working on that item until either it is complete or you can't work on it any more that day. Then move to number 2 and repeat the process, going down the list until the top 10 items have been completed done.

As for spending more time studying Internet marketing—if you know everything you need to know about Internet marketing from your studies, more power to you. If you don't, keep studying—but on your own time, not during your daily hour devoted to starting up your business.

Yes, there's always more to learn. But you'll learn it as you go along. And, because you'll actually be doing Internet marketing and not just reading about it, the lessons will stick better and be more meaningful to you.

Not to mention much more profitable.

7

Home-Based Business Opportunity #6: Close-Outs

All over the country, manufacturers and wholesalers have warehouses full of merchandise they cannot sell. If you run a close-out business, you can buy this merchandise for pennies on the dollar and sell it at a handsome profit either to retailers or direct to consumers.

Do you enjoy collecting various types of merchandise? Do you like to find bargains and buy products in mass quantities? Do you wish you had your own business selling what you find? Then you might consider opening a business where you can buy merchandise in bulk, at pennies on the retail dollar, and then resell your merchandise for a profit—even though you will still be selling at lower-than-retail prices.

Stores and businesses are always moving out seasonal and discounted merchandise from inventory. When a retail product is considered to be static, even at discounted prices, then the merchandise has to go somewhere to make room for new products. Rather than throwing everything into the dumpster and taking a loss, the retail store finds wholesale companies who will buy out the merchandise at the original price paid. If a business is closing down, then a liquidation company handles the buyout of the inventory and any office furnishings and equipment that need to be sold.

Is This for Me?

This type of business can be ideal for someone in the 50+ crowd who has some experience in retail or merchandising—or maybe just an eye for a good deal. By this point in your life, you have likely developed some strong interests and learned a lot about certain types of items and

Word to the Wise

Wholesale and liquidations companies are great for accessing close-out products if you want to buy very cheap and then resell your products online or through a bricks-and-mortar store. The more merchandise you buy in bulk, the greater discounts you'll get from the wholesale/liquidation company.

But beware of using a liquidation broker who does not personally own at least most of the merchandise you want to buy. Liquidation brokers will find merchandise at a great selling price, then search for a buyer willing to make the purchase quickly. The broker will add his fee onto the final purchasing price for his service in bringing together the wholesaler and buyer. But the broker cannot verify if the merchandise is in good shape and may not provide good service after the sale. So, be sure you know exactly who you are buying from.

have ideas about other people who would be interested in finding a good deal.

So, think first about what things interest you. Do you like motorcycles, deep sea fishing, boats, flying kites, swan figurines in all shapes and sizes, paintings, pictures, laptop computers? Make a list of each item or topic that interests you and then consider what types of merchandise go along with each topic that you could buy and sell. For instance, a close-out business is probably not going to be able to sell complete motorcycles, but you might be able to acquire and sell in-demand motorcycle parts, unusual bike accessories, distinctive biker jewelry and clothing, helmets, scratch-proof sunglasses, and riding boots.

Or, maybe you are fascinated with dragons and know lots of people who share your interest through multiple dragon fan-club groups you belong to. So, start looking for dragons in close-out offerings. In addition to dragon figurines, you might find close-out offerings of beautiful shelves with attached lighting that would display all the new figures.

You can also buy dragon pendants to resell. But you wouldn't think about selling dragon pendants without neck chains, would you? So look for deals on gold and silver chains. Or, consider finding bead kits in different colors that could be sold along with the pendants. Or, sell all the tools needed to make jewelry, like small pliers, wire clippers, beading trays, clasps, wire and ribbons rolls, hot glue guns, bead needles, and unusual jewelry pieces which can be incorporated into jewelry designs for additional accents. Along with the pendants, you can sell earrings and bracelets, toe rings, finger rings, belly button jewelry, belts, and even clothing. What about dragon stationery and cards?

The truth is, you can have a close-out business built around one theme or product, which can then be expanded to all kinds of extra sales to interested buyers and collectors.

FINDING YOUR MARKET

Based on what you'd like to sell, do you have a market in mind? Collectors are always a good place to start if you're selling unusual items. More mundane merchandise can be marketed to operations that need a lot of what you're selling. For example, hospitals and day care centers might be interested in buying discounted diapers and other baby items, as they use these products daily.

You might find that specialty retail stores are an ideal customer base. If you can find the type of merchandise carried in the stores, you can sell it to them in quantity to multiply your profits. For instance, a local store sells products for families with new babies. A manufacturer is getting rid of last year's strollers to make room for the new models. The strollers had a wholesale price of $200 each, but he offers to sell them to you for $50 each. You turn around and sell to the retail store for $100 each, making a 100 percent profit on your investment.

Or you can use eBay to sell your close-out wares. See Chapter 5 for more details about setting up a business selling on eBay.

DELIVERING THE GOODS

If you are planning to purchase large quantities of close-out merchandise, you need to think about where you will store it. Can it fit in your garage? Maybe you need to rent a storage space? Or, maybe you need a whole warehouse.

Alternatively, you may want to hire a company that handles drop shipping for you, so that you don't ever have to physically handle the merchandise or ship it out yourself. If you work with a drop ship business, you can focus on marketing, advertising, and finding customers who will purchase your products. You would forward all orders to the drop ship company, which will take care of storing, packaging, and postal costs for your products.

You can also be the drop ship company yourself if other businesses or websites are selling your products for you. Once they take the order and send you the money minus their percentage, you would then ship the item out of your warehouse, storage room, or garage, and you take the profit. Your available physical resources will determine that way you want to set your business up. If, for example, you are working out of an apartment, chances are good that you will be using a drop ship company to handle all the product fulfillment and shipping for you.

Finding Your Products

To find what close-out merchandise is available on the market, search the Internet for "close-out sales." You will find a long list of different companies that handle buy-outs and liquidations of many businesses and retail stores. Check each site to see what you can buy. You can often buy individual pieces or you can buy in bulk, maybe by the pallet, depending on the type of merchandise and available shipping arrangement and your own storage capacity.

The list below shows specials available by the pallet that were listed recently by a close-out specialist. This list will give you an idea of what kinds of merchandise might be available this way.

- Art/pictures/frames
- Housewares
- Automotive products
- Jeans
- Baby goods
- Lingerie
- Bed, bath, and linens
- Luggage
- Blinds and drapes
- Men's apparel
- Books
- Mixed apparel

- Children's apparel
- Mixed hard goods
- Computers
- Office loads
- Cosmetics/fragrances
- Pet products
- Costume jewelry
- Rugs
- Dollar store items
- Shoes/athletic footwear
- Domestic goods
- Socks
- Drugstore items
- Soft goods
- Electronics
- Sporting goods
- Fashion accessories
- Sports/toys/infants
- Nonperishable food products
- T-shirts
- Furniture
- Tools and paint
- General merchandise
- Toys
- Gifts/collectibles
- Used apparel/shoes
- Handbags and purses
- Women's apparel

This list is based on top-selling items that, in most cases, can be moved out quickly. The highest-moving sales are of electronic products, such as televisions, stereos, video game consoles, computers, laptops, GPS systems, netbooks (small laptops), and DVD and Blu-ray disc players. Also high in demand are baby items (there will always be babies!), cosmetics, jewelry, and brand-name clothing. Many of these brand names can be purchased for as much as 85 percent off the final retail price.

If you have something specific you'd like to sell—such as dragon figurines—then do an Internet search for "dragon figurine close-outs" to obtain a list of wholesale and liquidation companies handling dragon figurines. Your job now is to research which ones give you the best value for the amounts you want to purchase. It depends on the volume of your potential market, how much you want to invest, and the initial start-up quantity. This information will help you choose which company will provide the best services to you for your situation.

The other side of this business is to be the wholesale company, or liquidator, that buys directly from the business moving out the merchandise or closing down. This position requires a slightly different set of business rules and may be harder to do on your own. You most certainly would need to make sure your legal and financial foundation is structured correctly to handle this side of the operation, so consult a lawyer who is proficient in retail and wholesale laws if you are interested in pursuing this opportunity.

BEFORE YOU BUY

If you want to go into this type of business from either side, you will need to do significant research before opening up your doors, as several issues need to be covered before you start. Once you have a pretty good idea of what you want to sell, and have an idea of how to sell it, determine what business and legal issues you need to investigate before getting started. Don't spend a dime on inventory until you've covered everything on paper and have your business foundation arranged. Prepare a basic marketing plan as well as a business plan and take both to a lawyer and a certified public accountant (CPA) for review. You don't want to have any ugly surprises after getting underway and find yourself unable to back out without severe fines or financial loss.

If you have never negotiated or haggled over prices, or been in any type of retail sales environment before, you might want to take some classes on selling and negotiating. The object is to build working relationships with the companies that handle the merchandise you want. The more you work (sincerely) with your suppliers, the easier the process becomes over time. With knowledge, you will be able to bargain for lower prices in a competent and confident manner.

One of the best ways to learn about this business (or any business) is to contact those already in it. Ask people in the business where to go for more information and to find other businesses that help out wholesalers and liquidators.

Many online wholesale and liquidation companies have communities and blogs you can join where you can interact with other members to ask questions and share notes and stories about the close-out business. Blogs will be one of your most up-to-date methods of finding out all about your business and what is happening in the markets. You can find out what companies to avoid, or to patronize, based on feedback in the blogs and message lists. Additionally, you can do preliminary online marketing by listing your business on many of these sites, particularly when you are operating in a niche area.

Of course, you will need a website for your business. Study other close-out websites to see how they are set up and how easy it is to find information. Also, check out their setup for ease in making a purchase. One of the most important aspects of your website is to make it easy to complete a purchase in record time. It is vital that the process be easy and efficient or you will lose customers who don't have the patience to spend time running around your website.

Study the websites for 10 to 20 wholesalers, close-outs, and liquidations. Take notes on each site about graphics, copywriting, advertising, appeal, colors and backgrounds, and also find out what company built the site for the business. Scroll to the bottom of the page, find the webmaster/designer link, and click on it to get reference information. If you see that many of the websites are designed by the same person or company, you know you are on to something. Do not leave your commercial lifeline website in the hands of an amateur, or you are likely to fail before getting out of the starting gate!

Depending on what kind of merchandise you are selling, you will certainly need to have good photos of your products that you can put online. Unless you are exceptional with a camera, consider hiring a good photographer to do a shoot with all your products. While it will be an outlay of money, you will recoup this in sales returns. If you have a warehouse full of rare antiques, you will definitely need to provide pictures that will help sell your treasures for you.

Everything you do in this business is about buying at the lowest price and then reselling for the best price you can get, while still providing good deals to your customers. Knowing what you're doing and knowing what your market can provide can help you create a true win-win situation for you AND your customers. That is why you want to be in this business. You can make money and help others at the same time.

STRAIGHT TALK FROM BOB

I know a lot of rich people—a slew of hard-driving individuals whose wealth and accomplishments put the rest of the population to shame.

And I've spent a lot of my life—too much, in fact—comparing myself to them … and of course, coming up short.

So, I'm not going to do it any more.

And neither should you.

If you judge yourself only in comparison to others—who they are, what they have, what they've done—you can always find someone who outperforms you in any given area.

We obsess about those who are "greater" and feel bad that we don't measure up to their success and accomplishments. Psychologists call this unhealthy obsession "compare despair."

So, what can you do about it?

To begin with, stop comparing yourself to others. Unless you're Bill Gates, there's always someone who makes more money than you.

Unless you're George Clooney or Jessica Alba, there's always someone either more famous or better looking—or both.

So quit worrying about how you stack up against other people. Instead, figure out what's important to you—helping others in need, writing good books or great copy, being a terrific parent, becoming a guru in your industry or market niche, teaching, or giving your clients a level of service they can't get anywhere else.

Then, when you know you've made the absolute best effort you can in pursuit of these objectives, take a minute to feel good about yourself.

After all, you deserve it.

8

Home-Based Business Opportunity #7: Import/Export

Fluctuations in the value of the American dollar against foreign currencies create continual opportunities for profits in an import/export business. Although this type of business may not be one of the first that comes to mind when you think about setting up a home-based business, this chapter will give you some ideas about why an import/export business could be a good opportunity for you and will give you some ideas about how to start one.

Starting an Import Business

Are you looking for a business that could realistically bring in $50,000 or more a year? One highly lucrative option for the entrepreneurs among us is to start a business as a U.S. importer.

Countries around the globe have goods they wish to sell at a low, low price. Relatively wealthy Americans are looking to buy those same goods at a fair market price. When you become the "middle man," connecting the buyers to the sellers, you can benefit by earning a portion of the sale price.

If you do this right, you can earn a substantial income. Importing is big business in America today. The U.S. Department of Commerce estimates that $1.2 trillion in goods are imported into the United States annually, and many of those imports are handled through small businesses, not the "big-box" retailers. The Department of Commerce reports that only about 4 percent of all the dealers who are in this business are the "big" retailers. Most in the import/export business are small businesses.

But be aware that starting an importing business can seem overwhelming. Without the right guidance, you could invest thousands of dollars in a business that never takes off. This chapter aims to shed some light on the world of importing.

Is This for Me?

While setting up and running an importing business is not terribly difficult, it is not the right business venture for everyone. First, you need to realize that it does require some selling. Even if you are selling online, where you can be fairly anonymous, you are still selling. People over 50 who have spent decades perfecting the art of the sale could find this part of running an import business invigorating and exciting. But if you have never been in sales and are not willing to learn how to make a sales pitch, find another business venue.

Second, you must be fairly organized to succeed in this business. You will be receiving, sending, and tracking valuable shipments on a regular basis, so you must understand how to keep good records. If you don't mind sales and can be organized, you could be a good fit for this business.

The importing business is not highly expensive to start, but you will need some capital to get up and running, which is another reason it might be a great opportunity for people over 50, who frequently have access to more capital than a younger entrepreneur would.

The business can be pretty simple and straightforward; you will not need to rent an office or storefront, and you will not need many, if any, employees. You also will not want a tremendous amount of inventory in the beginning. All of these positive facets can make this kind of opportunity ideal for someone over 50 who wants to open a home-based business.

Start-Up Costs

Take some time to calculate your start-up expenses before you begin. Whether you decide you need only $5,000 for your first shipment or you want more so that you can establish a working website, set up a steady supply chain, and secure storage facilities, let's consider some ideas to help you get your hands on that money.

One option is to use a portion of your savings or retirement funds. This is not ideal for most start-up businesses, particularly if you are over 50 and nearing the age when you will need those retirement funds. Before you even consider drawing from your savings in that way, make sure you have done your research and be certain that you have a good market for the products that you are going to import.

Another option is to open a line of credit at your bank. If you have a good credit rating and a strong relationship with the bank, this should be a possibility. If you own your house, you might be able to take out a second mortgage or home equity line of credit to help you finance some of the items you will need to successfully start your business.

What Goods Can Be Imported

Before you begin a business buying overseas merchandise and selling it locally, you must understand that all goods are subject to import/export laws. These laws govern what can and cannot be brought into the United States and resold. Some goods are prohibited altogether, while others are heavily taxed, which could eat up your profits. In general, products that are banned from being imported into the United States are those that would harm the public or the wildlife of the country or in any other way hurt the nation's interests.

To have a successful importing business, you must find a product that is legal to import and involves few, if any, regulations. You should also be aware that laws about what can be imported change frequently, so you need to consistently keep up with new laws or regulations that would affect your business. The following list shows common items people may consider importing, although you should always check for federal, state, and local laws concerning any imports.

Alcoholic beverages. If you intend to import alcoholic beverages, check with your state's alcoholic beverage control board to ensure that the product is compliant with your state's laws and regulations.

Ceramics. Ceramics have no restrictions, but you may wish to proceed with caution if you're looking at ceramic tableware. Some foreign-made products are glazed with a product containing high levels of lead, which could contaminate food and beverages and put your customers at risk. Consider having ceramic tableware tested for lead content, particularly if it is purchased from Mexico, China, Hong Kong, or India.

Firearms and ammunition. While you may know of a huge market for firearms and ammunition, this option might not be the best option as an import business. Many weapons are banned completely. Certain weapons are allowed as imports, but only through a licensed importer, dealer, or manufacturer. Working with a "middle man" or becoming licensed yourself can cut into your profits.

Food products. Prepared food products, like bakery items, candies, condiments, packaged spices, coffee, tea, and even some cheeses, are permitted as imports. Items containing meat products are almost always prohibited. Keep in mind that the U.S. Food and Drug Administration (FDA) does place additional regulations on some food products, so check before you attempt to import such an item.

Textiles/other goods. Some textiles and other products may have to meet the standards of their particular regulatory agencies in order to be imported into the U.S. These include art supplies; toxic, flammable, or hazardous materials; household appliances; certain electronics; and toys and other items for children.

Once you choose the product you want to import, make sure you thoroughly research all rules and regulations surrounding that item before you take the next step.

Word to the Wise

As you choose items for your import business, always consider the duty imposed on them when you import them. The United States International Trade Commission keeps a database of current tariff rates that you can use to research this cost. You will find this database at http://dataweb.usitc.gov/scripts/tariff_current.asp.

Finding Merchandise to Import

The first step in becoming a successful importer is choosing your product. This will dictate the direction your business takes, including where you will sell your goods and where you will buy them. Your goal in finding merchandise to import is two-fold. First, you need a product that fills a unique niche. Perhaps there is a huge market for a particular gizmo, but if that market is already saturated with resellers, you will struggle to make a profit.

Second, you need a product that you can sell for a profit. This means there needs to be enough of a difference between the price you pay for the items and the price you can sell them for to allow you to bring home a profit after paying your expenses.

There are three ways an imported product can bring a higher sales price than its purchase price. The first is if the import is very rare in a particular geographic area. The second is if it is prestigious simply because of its location of origin. The third, and perhaps most common, is if the item is particularly cheap when purchased overseas.

Choosing your item requires spending some time researching the various opportunities for importing. You will need to scour the Internet and talk to other importers to see what products are hot and are easy to import.

DOING MARKET RESEARCH

Before you fall in love with the idea of importing a particular item, take the time to do some market research. Is there a market for the product? Is there room for profit? As you do an in-depth study of the market, keep these considerations in mind:

Define your target market. Who will buy the product? Will you market to individual consumers, industrial suppliers, or the government? What is each prospective customer's budget like? Where do your potential customers shop? What do they do for work or fun?

What will set the product you want to sell apart from other similar products?

Which country or countries will you import from?

How will you sell the product (your trade channel)?

The answers to these questions will help you narrow down your product options to just a few items.

FINDING A PARTNER

Once you are certain what type of products you want to sell, it is time to find an actual supplier.

The most affordable way to import items is to buy them directly from the manufacturer. Any time you add another company (middleman) into the process, you will lose potential income. Scour the Internet to look for manufacturers of the product you have chosen in the area where you wish to buy the item.

As you are looking for a list of companies willing to work with your business, check out these directories:

- http://b2b.tradeholding.com/default.cgi/action/directory/view/companies/
- http://www.importers.com

When you contact an international manufacturer, make sure that your business communications look professional, even if you are just starting out. Order professional letterhead and stationery and use it to represent your business. Consider using gold leaf to make it look even more professional. Mail an inquiry letter to the manufacturer, stating your intentions and desire to sell its products.

Here is another advantage someone over 50 may have in establishing this kind of business. You've had quite a few years to establish business and personal relationships; maybe you've traveled extensively in certain countries or lived overseas for a few years; maybe you have family members who live overseas now. You should draw upon all those relationships and acquaintances as you start looking for suppliers.

You can mail letters or use e-mail as you try to establish initial contact with businesses; maybe you should do both. Don't just pick out one or two promising manufacturers; send dozens or hundreds of inquiry letters or e-mails to potential manufacturers until you get a positive response. Whether you use mail or e-mail, your communication should introduce your company, ask for the name and information for a potential contact within the business, and request any information about other firms in related areas they might know that you could contact. This process can take some time, but, with persistence, you will find a company who is willing to sell you its items at wholesale cost.

Consider using a questionnaire with your letter. This will invite a response from interested trade partners. Ask about goods they want to export. Find out about any products they manufacture that are currently being imported by others. How are they distributed? Are there representatives or sales branches in other cities? What is the history of the company? Do they have a catalog or sample they could send to you?

You will want to send hundreds of these inquiries, because many will not provide a response. From the responses you do receive, choose several companies that look to be the most promising and follow up with further contact.

Use all available resources to research companies you are interested in. Foreign consulates in the United States are a good place to learn of businesses that are looking to establish a market in the United States through importers like you. You can also talk with representatives at U.S. embassies in the country with which you intend to do business to gain further information. The embassy is also a good resource as you research the reputation and history of a particular business. Always thoroughly research a potential trade partner before entering into an agreement or making a purchase.

Another option is to work through a wholesale distributor. Many wholesalers will sell bulk orders of a particular item at a price much lower than retail. Be careful, however, when choosing a wholesaler, and do not take their word about price savings. Often, they inflate the actual retail price of the item. Do your own research to determine whether or not you will make a profit when reselling the items at the current retail price.

Finding a Country

After you have chosen an item you want to import, think about from which country you should buy the item. Some items are more valuable when they come from a particular place simply because people *think*

How Bob Does It

One area of uncertainty among almost all entrepreneurs is how often to follow up with prospects.

Fail to do so often enough and you may lose an opportunity to another vendor who is more visible. Do so too often and you risk being an annoyance.

One technique that helps is to make sure you are NOT being a pest when you follow up.

Whether I am following up by phone or e-mail, the first thing I say is "I don't want to be a pest, but ...", followed by a brief description of why I am calling.

This works amazingly well. Almost without fail, the prospect replies, "You're not being a pest—I am glad you followed up!"

I don't know what about "I don't want to be a pest, but" works. I only know that it works like magic.

they are. Caviar, for instance, is more prestigious when it comes from an exotic location than when harvested domestically. Other goods are better purchased overseas because they are cheap and you can sell them for a good profit. China and Taiwan, for instance, often have cheap electronics, household goods, and toys that can be resold for a profit.

These are the top trading partners of the United States in order from largest amount of import and export dollars to smallest:

- Canada
- Mexico
- Japan
- China
- Germany
- United Kingdom
- France
- South Korea
- Taiwan
- Singapore

Once you have determined the item you are going to sell, check the availability of exporters from these countries to see if they can sell you the product at a good price. But keep in mind that these are not your only options when it comes to choosing an exporting country. Just remember that any country under a trade embargo is off-limits for importers.

Getting Deeper Discounts

The goal of an importing business is to buy low and sell high. The deeper the discounts you can obtain on the products you are purchasing, the higher your potential profit will be.

The deepest discounts are almost always given on bulk orders, so to get the deepest discounts, you may have to buy a large number of items at a time. Shop with many different manufacturers, and do not be afraid to pit them against one another. For instance, let manufacturer A know what manufacturer B is offering and see if they will match or lower their price. Bartering is usually essential to getting the deepest discounts on the items you will be selling.

Dealing with Customs

As you import goods, you will need to learn to deal properly with customs. When your items arrive on U.S. soil, they will not be sent directly to you. They will be held at the mail branch until all customs forms have been filled out and all fees or duties have been paid. You will be informed that the parcels have arrived. What you are importing and where your products came from will dictate how you must clear customs. Be sure you check with customs and know exactly what will be required before you start. Laws and regulations change, so be sure to look for the latest guidelines.

While dealing with customs may seem like a hassle, it really requires little more than some time and paperwork—and up-to-date knowledge. Once you have done it a few times, it will feel no different than taking a trip to the post office to ask that your mail be held when you go on vacation. Simply be honest, pay the applicable fees in a timely manner, and you will be able to breeze through customs without hassle.

Pricing Your Merchandise

Now that you have your items safely in hand, you are ready to sell them. The first step in selling is setting your price, which requires some detailed research.

In general, you should look to bring in 10 percent above your wholesale cost when you sell the item. So, on an item that you bought for $100, you should get a $10 commission when all is finalized. This may not seem like much, but you must remember that you will be selling hundreds if not thousands of items, so the money adds up quickly.

However, remember to consider your expenses when deciding on the selling price. A selling price of $110 is usually not sufficient on an item that cost you $100. You will lose money if you use this as the selling price, because you will not have any money to put toward overhead.

What type of overhead should you consider when factoring your expenses? The answer will vary tremendously, based on how your business is set up. Here are some common sources of overhead for U.S. importers, above the purchase cost:

- Duties paid on the items
- Insurance

- Shipping
- Special packaging
- eBay fees
- Website hosting costs
- Website maintenance costs
- Office supplies
- Fax, computer, phone, Internet service, and other technology-related expenses

Try to determine how much of the overhead applies to each individual item and then add that to your $110 figure. This will give you an idea of the price you should charge. Finally, check your competition to make sure that your price is still reasonable. If you find that your price is still much lower than the competition, you can raise it a bit to increase your commission.

Selling Your Merchandise—In a Store

Once you have your product, you need to find a way to sell it. The first option many people consider is selling their goods in a store. This can be profitable, if you know how to do it right.

One easy way to sell your goods is to sell them on consignment. Find a shop that is interested in the product you are offering, and then put some of your items up for sale on a consignment basis. When the item sells, you will receive a portion of the selling price based on a set percentage. This will only work if your markup is high enough for the consignment shop to keep its cut and still give you a decent profit.

You may need to help with marketing when selling items on consignment, because you may have to set up the display, keep the product stocked, and even refer people to the store to buy your products. Usually, locally owned stores are the ones that will be most willing to work with importers to sell goods on consignment.

To offer your items on consignment through a store, you need a consignment agreement with the merchant. Such an agreement should cover the following four items:

INVENTORY. Your consignment agreement should contain a listing of all of the items you are offering for sale, including quantities, descriptions, and retail price.

SALES SPLIT. How will the sale be split between you and the store? The more you get, the better, so shop around for a store with a split that is highly in your favor. Be sure to get the details in writing.

PAYMENT SCHEDULE. You should have an agreement in writing as to when and how you will be paid.

DURATION OF CONSIGNMENT. The agreement should discuss the length of time your items will be offered for sale. If your items do not sell in this period of time, the store can either offer you a new consignment agreement or return your items to you.

If you choose to place your items in a store on consignment, always remember that the items belong to you until they sell. If you come to believe that the store is not the right place for your items, you are free to remove them and try another store.

Another option is to sell the items in bulk to a store. You will be offering the items at a "wholesale" price, which is still lower than the retail price a customer will pay. In return for receiving a lower price, the store agrees to buy a large number of your items. Once the purchase is made, you are done with the items. They become the property of the store and the store will be responsible for marketing and selling the items.

Larger stores with a bigger buying budget offer your best chances to sell your items in bulk. Keep in mind that you will need a strong niche to be able to sell in this way, because most of the big-box stores will have their own international suppliers for a particular product. Unless you have a strong niche product, you will struggle to make money by selling in bulk to retailers.

There is less paperwork involved when you sell items wholesale. You simply sell the items, offer a receipt, and take your money. There is no need for an agreement, unless you plan to enter into an ongoing trade relationship, because the items become the property of the store once the sale is complete.

To find stores interested in buying wholesale products from you, go through the same process you did when you were looking for suppliers. Send out hundreds of contact letters, introducing your business and your product. Chances are high that you will hear back from some of these contacts, earning yourself a new business partner. Do not limit yourself when sending out these letters. A letter costs little to mail, but a good contact can be invaluable when you work as an importer.

Selling Your Goods—Online

Small business importers most often sell their goods via the Internet. Selling imports through online platforms makes the entire country your target market, because you are limited geographically only through shipping costs. To sell things online, you have two basic options: to use auction sites or to sell from your own stand-alone website.

Auction Sites

Selling via auction sites, the most popular of which is eBay, is quite lucrative for many people. You save yourself the hassle and expense of setting up and managing your own website, while opening your products to a global market with little advertising expense on your part. Many people turn to eBay and similar auction sites when searching for affordable goods, and if the product you are importing happens to be one that auction users often search for, you have a readily available market. The auction site will do your marketing for you, and all you have to do is list your goods for sale. If you wish to sell things on eBay, knowing how to use the site before you begin is essential to your success. See Chapter 5 in this book for more details about selling on eBay.

Once you have listed your auction, monitor it carefully. Answer any buyer questions, and ship promptly once the item has sold. This will help you gain more positive feedback as you work to establish your niche.

Personal Sites

Setting up your personal online store is a bit more work-intensive. First, you will need to choose a host for your website. This is the company that keeps your website's information on its computers and ensures that information is always available. Next, choose a domain name—something that is easy for users to remember and that also applies well to your product and niche. Often, the website host will include domain registration in the cost of hosting a site.

Many hosts also have tools you can use to help you set up your online store. Choose a host with store-friendly features like e-commerce packages and ready-to-use website templates. Because you will be taking money through your site, choose a host that is secure and provides SSL encryption. Learn more about creating your own website and using it wisely in Chapter 10.

Where to Turn for Help

If you find that you need some help along the way in establishing and operating your business as an importer, there are resources available to you. Check the Resources section at the end of this book for some ideas about where to find help.

Remember, there will a period of trial and error as you enter this—or any—new business endeavor, but overall you will find it rewarding and profitable if you find the right product and the right market. So, get out there and start researching. Good luck!

STRAIGHT TALK FROM BOB

During my three decades as a copywriter, I have observed that business owners and managers fall into one of four categories as far as their competence and skill in marketing is concerned.

By recognizing which category you are in and taking the action steps recommended below, you can move up to the next level and significantly increase the return on investment from your marketing investment, no matter what kind of business you are running.

The lowest level of marketing competence is ***unconscious incompetence***. You don't know what you are doing and, worse, you don't know that you don't know. You may think you are a pretty sharp marketer, even though to others that is clearly not the case. Egotistical small business owners who appear in their own TV commercials and junior employees at "creative" Madison Avenue ad agencies can fall into this category.

Do you think you are an okay marketer, and you always blame the lack of results generated by your marketing on external factors, such as bad timing, bad lists, or bad luck? You are probably in the unconscious incompetence stage. Recognize that you don't know what you're doing, and it is hurting your business. Get help. Hire a marketing manager who knows more than you do. Or, take a marketing course or workshop.

The next stage up the ladder is ***conscious incompetence***. You've recognized that the reason your marketing isn't working is that you don't know what you're doing. Again, take the steps listed above.

When I was at this stage as an advertising manager who had recently graduated from college and had only a year of work experience under my belt (instead of the considerable paunch that resides there now), I hired an experienced ad agency and leaned on them for guidance.

This strategy worked well for me and my employer. The company got better advertising than I could have produced on my own. And, working with the agency accelerated my own marketing education, making me a more valuable employee.

Moving higher up the ladder of marketing competence, you reach the stage of ***conscious competence***. You've read the books, taken the courses, and understand what works. But your experience at putting it into practice is limited. That means whenever you want to create a product or service promotion, you have to slow down and think about what you are doing. It doesn't come naturally.

In this stage, you should keep checklists, formulas, and swipe files (examples of successful promotions you admire) close at hand. Model your own efforts after the winners of others. Don't try to reinvent the wheel. Observe what works and adapt it to your own product and market.

Do this enough times, and you will slowly begin to become a true master of marketing. You will reach the highest level of marketing competence, ***unconscious competence***.

At this stage, coming up with great offers, promotional ideas, headlines, and copy is second nature to you. You do it naturally, without having to consult your checklists or reference files. The quality of your work is better, and it comes faster and easier.

However, you should still keep an extensive swipe file of promotions. Borrowing ideas and inspiration from promotions that are working is a time-honored tradition in our industry, as long as it does not step over into plagiarism or copyright infringement.

My colleague Michael Masterson says it takes approximately 1,000 hours of practice to become really competent at copywriting, marketing, playing the flute, or anything else. If you have expert guidance, you may be able to cut that to 500 hours.

But ultimately, you learn by doing—and doing a lot. If you are at this stage, keep doing more and more marketing. When you have put in 5,000 hours, you will become great, not just good, and your results will be even better.

9

Home-Based Business Opportunity #8: Real Estate

Despite the soft housing market that has existed in the United States since the late 2000s, real estate remains one of the best long-term investments, and people over 50 who want to start a home-based business should seriously—but realistically—consider a business involving real estate. In this chapter, you will learn about opportunities in the residential and commercial real estate markets and get a realistic view of the career opportunities in these business activities. You have heard and read a lot of negative evaluations of the real estate market the past few years, but when things seem the bleakest, you can often find the best opportunities. So, take a look and see if these areas might be of interest to you.

Is This for Me?

Everyone knows that real estate took a horrible hit in the late 2000s and has been struggling ever since. Most know that real estate has rebounded at least slightly since then and that hopeful signs have been starting to appear as of early 2013. But no one knows when the real estate market will really be healthy again. For every hopeful sign and optimistic study, you can find other worrisome trends and discouraging reports.

So anyone thinking about getting into real estate—as an investor or a realtor—has to research the most current reports and conditions and carefully consider if this is the right career path for you. Particularly if you are 50 or older, you need to understand how the ups and downs of the real estate market could affect your earning potential. If a down market hits after you have invested a lot of your time and money in real estate, you won't have as many years to recover as would someone in their 30s.

However, someone who is a little older and wiser may be better able to weather the storms that arise. A booming market can sometimes mislead younger entrepreneurs because they don't believe prices can go anywhere but up; they haven't seen the crashes you've seen, and so they may take more risks. But because you know prices go up AND down, you can be more deliberate about what risks you take; you may not earn as much as quickly in good times, but you could be the only one left standing if the good times come to a screeching halt.

With this economy, is it really a good time to become involved with the real estate business, particularly the residential part of the business? The answer is yes and no. Yes, if you are willing to devote the time and energy, believe in your ability to deal with a difficult economy, and understand that the weakened condition of a market usually occurs at the bottom of an economic cycle.

If you are looking for a secure career, there are others that offer more security but less opportunity. You may not be aware that a number of people made a lot of money and were very successful in real estate following the Great Depression in the 1930s.

What types of people succeed in real estate? According to the National Association of Realtors, nearly 70 percent of real estate sales agents came to the industry from unrelated fields, such as teaching, nursing, communications, government, retail, and the armed forces. Only about 25 percent had previously worked in a management or sales position.

Ultimately, this is a sales career, and there will be days when you may become frustrated or discouraged. But it is important to be able to remain positive and full of enthusiasm. By this point in your life, you should know whether this describes you or not.

Investing in Real Estate

The most recent data indicates that many consumers may be willing to begin spending again. In many areas of the country, foreclosures are down and home sales are up. But that doesn't mean that people have thrown caution to the wind and returned to spendthrift ways. As I write this, the 2012 elections have and the country is still coming to grips with the results and what they might mean for the country's economic future. Uncertainty remains over interest rates and taxes and whether current tax deductions that favor home owners will remain intact.

Any facts or figures that I could include here could very well be outdated by the time you pick up this book. So, if you are interested in a career in real estate investments—whether commercial or residential—you need to start by researching market and economic forecasts thoroughly. You may find that real estate in your area is a great buy—even if it is still suffering in the country overall. Or, you may discover that your area is still depressed when the rest of your state is rebounding.

Having more experience in a particular area can give you a distinct advantage over younger investors. If you have lived in your area for a long time, you may have lived through several real estate boom and bust cycles, and you may recognize the signs of a recovery even before they start to show up on the stat sheets. Or, you may have information about a particular business or industry in your area that you know is going to need more office space soon, and so you can start looking for suitable commercial property.

Word to the Wise

If you are interested in beginning a real estate career, start now to learn the business and develop relationships with real estate agencies and investment groups in your area that are encouraging and supportive of new participants. Learn about your local market and see if you find this type of work interesting and desirable before you sink a lot of money into it.

Starting a Career in Residential Real Estate

Selling real estate is a service business. The purchase of a home or property is one of the most important, complex, and significant financial events most people will ever make. Because of the complexity and importance of this transaction, people usually need help from real estate brokers and sales agents when considering the purchase or sale of a home.

Experienced real estate brokers and sales agents should have a comprehensive knowledge of the local real estate market and know which neighborhoods are best suited to the needs and budgets of their clients. They should also be familiar with local zoning and tax laws and know where to find financing for the purchase of property. Your age could definitely play to your advantage here—if you have lived in the same area for many years, you may be much more familiar with local laws and with the benefits and disadvantages of particular neighborhoods. That insider knowledge can be a big asset to a newcomer.

Brokers and Agents

So, what is the difference between a real estate broker and a real estate agent? While brokers and agents perform similar functions, they have different regulatory requirements. Brokers are licensed to manage their own real estate businesses. Agents are required to work with a broker and usually offer their services to a licensed real estate broker on a contractual basis.

When an agent sells a property, the broker pays the agent a portion of the commission earned from the sale of the property. Brokers can function independently or as part of a larger agency. In addition to selling real estate, brokers may also rent or manage properties for a fee.

As part of the sale process, it is not unusual for brokers and agents to provide information on the community, schools, churches, and stores in the area, as well as to spend a lot of time showing properties that they think will be suitable and appealing for their buyers.

Agents or brokers usually act as intermediaries in price negotiations between buyers and sellers and may help arrange financing for a prospective buyer that could mean the difference between success and failure in a sale. Brokers or agents order title searches to verify ownership and frequently meet with buyers and sellers to work out the details of a sales agreement. In some cases, brokers and agents may assume primary responsibility for finalizing or closing a transaction, but lenders or lawyers usually perform this function.

If you are an agent or broker, an important part of your daily activity is to look for properties to buy or sell, but your primary job is to solve problems for your clients. Good agents have some idea about how much it will cost to replace a 50-year-old furnace, upgrade an electrical system, line a chimney, or replace a worn-out roof. They also know reliable service personnel who can provide prospective buyers with more details about these types of repairs.

Agents usually meet with prospective buyers to discuss what they are looking for in a house. Then come numerous appointments with the buyers to visit available properties that the agent considers to be within the parameters of what the clients are seeking in a house. In the process of completing a sale, the agent acts as a representative of the buyer and/or seller and must follow a client's instructions precisely when presenting offers or counteroffers.

In many instances, brokers and agents must deal with environmental issues, such as advising buyers if there is lead paint in the walls and ensuring that any legally mandated or agreed-upon inspections, such as termite and radon inspections, take place. While mortgage loan officers, attorneys, or escrow officers handle many of the financial and legal details, the agent must ensure that all terms of a sales contract are met before the closing, including any required repairs.

If you are a real estate agent, you will need to work with a broker or brokerage firm, and it's important to find a brokerage where you are comfortable and can work with people who have attitudes similar to yours.

With the advances in telecommunications and the ability to retrieve data about properties over the Internet, many real estate brokers and sales agents prefer to work out of their homes instead of a real estate office. No matter where they set up shop, agents spend much of their time away from their desks, showing properties to customers, analyzing properties for sale, meeting with prospective clients, or researching the local market.

TRAINING AND QUALIFICATIONS

Every state and the District of Columbia require real estate brokers and sales agents to be licensed. To obtain a license, prospective brokers and agents must pass a written examination that is more comprehensive for brokers than for agents. It covers the basic real estate transactions and the state laws affecting the sale of property.

Most states require candidates for the sales agent license to complete between 30 and 90 hours of classroom instruction. For a broker's license, an individual must have between 60 and 90 hours of formal training and one to three years of real estate sales experience. Some states waive the experience requirement for a broker's license if the applicant has a bachelor's degree in real estate.

Typically, state licenses must be renewed every one or two years, usually without an examination, but many states require continuing education for license renewals.

While agents and brokers must be high school graduates, a large number have college degrees. As real estate transactions have become more legally and financially complex, some firms have turned entirely to college graduates to fill positions.

In most states, members of the National Association of Realtors sponsor courses covering both the fundamentals and legal aspects of the field. In addition, some of the larger brokerage firms offer formal training programs for both beginners and experienced agents.

However, much of the early training necessary to learn the practical aspects of the business is conducted on the job under the direction of an experienced broker or agent.

Real Estate Career Pitfalls and Considerations

You should be aware that there is a high degree of turnover in the business and that approximately 70 percent, or more, of new agents don't make it in the first year. So, you need to be realistic when you enter the business. This is not a part-time job, and you should be fully committed to devote the time necessary to succeed.

It is not unusual for residential real estate agents and brokers to work evenings and weekends for the convenience of their clients. During your first years, you will have to devote a fair amount of time to meeting with prospective clients and showing houses. The more interest and concern you show for your prospects, the better your chance of success. Proving your concern, however, can mean dropping everything to meet with a client or making phone calls on a client's behalf.

Working these kinds of hours and having this schedule variability may actually be easier for you to do at your stage in life than it is for agents who have young kids at home. If you're willing to put in long hours and be highly flexible, you have a higher likelihood to succeed and will put yourself in a better position to earn a high level of income. Eventually, if you are successful in the business for a few years, you can earn the right to be less available.

Personality Required

Personality traits may be as important as academic background to achieving success in real estate. Brokers look for agents who have a pleasant personality and a neat appearance. Maturity, good judgment, trustworthiness, honesty, and enthusiasm for the job are required to attract prospective customers in this highly competitive field.

Agents should be well organized and detail oriented and have a good memory for names, faces, and business particulars. A good knowledge of the local area and its neighborhoods is a distinct advantage.

By now, you know whether you have the characteristics it takes to effectively sell real estate. You've probably worked in a variety of settings and offices and you know whether you enjoy interacting one-on-one or prefer to sit in the back office and crunch numbers. Plus, you most likely have learned a lot about people, and you can quickly size up a potential client and know what it will take to help that person. You can use all this knowledge to your advantage if you decide selling real estate is a good career option for you at this stage of your life.

If you do decide to enter the real estate business, you should know that about 60 percent of real estate brokers and sales agents are self-employed and that some of these work part-time by combining their real estate activities with other careers. While real estate is sold in all areas of the country, most agents work in large urban areas and rapidly growing communities.

How Bob Does It

One of my subscribers recently wrote to me that "These days, trust is the ultimate Unique Selling Proposition," a sentiment I completely agree with.

Trust is especially difficult to build in my field of Internet marketing, where consumers perceive that many of the marketers are con men and hucksters. It can also be hard to build trust as a realtor or real estate investor for the same reasons.

The following are some things I do in my Internet information marketing business that I hope build my subscribers' trust in me. Most of these practices could be modified to use in real estate or most any field:

- I promptly honor all requests for refunds, even if a customer requests a refund after the 90-day deadline has passed.
- I keep my product prices fair and modest.
- We respond to all e-mails. If it's a marketing question, I answer it personally.
- I am easy to get into contact with; for example, I pick up my own phone.
- My information products are accurately presented, as far as I know. Not because I know everything, but because I only write or record information products on topics I have first-hand experience with.
- My writing reflects my personality. Subscribers to my newsletter feel they have gotten to know me.
- My e-mails and websites are purposefully low key. The more you use hype in your copy, the less people trust you.
- I don't brag endlessly to readers about my money or my houses or my cars or our vacations. People dislike braggarts.
- I do not have a big ego. This, too, endears me to subscribers.
- I give away a lot of valuable free content in my e-mails and on my various websites.
- I have written 80 books published by trade publishers. This credential validates me as an expert in the eyes of some readers.
- I have 33 years experience in marketing. My longevity reassures some people that I know what I am doing.
- I am 55 years old. My gray hairs are a comfort for baby boomers and others who are distrustful of the very young and inexperienced.
- I have an enormous collection of testimonials on my website.

A Career in Commercial Real Estate

While there are similar activities involved in residential and commercial real estate sales, the differences are significant. Making a living while selling commercial real estate is generally much more demanding than it is in the residential market.

When you are selling a home to a couple, locating the right home is the biggest part of the job. They fall in love with it on their own. Not so with a commercial buyer or lease client.

A great deal more research is required—including financial analysis, market demographics study, and environmental research—in a typical commercial purchase or lease decision. The commercial client is usually much more concerned with area statistics and data about the property's location and the demographics of the local population and businesses.

The average day's activities for a commercial real estate broker can be quite different from those of the residential agent. Here are a few of the activities you may find on your task list for the day:

- Cold calls on business managers and owners
- Study of the lease payments for office complexes in the area
- Calculation of the break-even ratio for a commercial property
- Interpretation of current lease rates and practices for a prospective multi-family property buyer
- Report of population growth for likely patients at a medical rental complex
- Cap rate report for a prospective buyer of a small shopping center

As you can see, this list includes activities that never come up for a residential real estate agent.

There is a higher level of analytical activity for the typical commercial real estate professional. The rewards can be worth the effort required, but you should thoroughly compare your desires and abilities to the requirements for commercial real estate sales. You should know by now whether you have the skills and personality to provide the services required in this field.

Reserve Required

Unlike in residential real estate, the commercial real estate agent cannot count on a fast start by working with friends and relatives. They aren't usually buying or leasing offices or retail spaces.

Trying to learn this new profession will prove to be very stressful if you are overly concerned about paying next month's bills. Unless your current sphere of influence is made up mostly of businesspeople, it's likely that your start in commercial real estate will be a gradual one. Be prepared to spend a lot of time and energy learning the business.

If you have been working in residential real estate, very little of what you did there will be a big help in the commercial arena. Everything from clients to property types to contracts and documents are very different.

If you have a sufficient financial reserve, you will experience less stress and can focus on getting your feet wet in commercial real estate. If your goal is to be a commercial real estate agent or broker, having held a full-time position with a commercial brokerage firm will certainly help prepare you for what you need to set up your own business.

Confidence and Patience Required, Too

Unlike in residential real estate, the typical commercial client isn't as emotionally involved in the process. You cannot make a living just showing properties until the client goes, "I love it … this is the one!"

Instead, you'll likely be dealing with a businessperson who will be much more analytical and who will want a great deal more due diligence from a real estate professional. Prospect-to-closing usually takes much longer in commercial real estate. If you are into immediate gratification, you probably won't enjoy working in commercial real estate.

Be sure that you'll be patient enough to work with a client for months and offer a great deal of research and property analysis before an offer is even considered. Then, after the offer, the process of due diligence remains much more involved in commercial property transfers than in residential transfers.

Commercial real estate can be quite lucrative if that's your cup of tea. The commercial real estate agent must be willing to work hard, be quite aggressive, and above all, be intelligent and very competent in the special skills required for this niche. It's different, but if commercial real estate is for you, the rewards can be great.

If you are interested in commercial real estate property management, the Commercial Investment Real Estate Institute (CIREI), through its education program, has been conferring the Certified Commercial Investment Member (CCIM) designation since 1969.

Careers in Other Areas of Real Estate

There are other opportunities to start a business in real estate. Most of these niche areas require some specialty knowledge and experience, which you may have acquired from years of work experience or perhaps through years of pursuing a particular hobby, repairing your own home, or managing your own investments. Consider all the knowledge and experience you have acquired, both formally and informally, and think about whether you could put that to work in one of these areas.

Farm and Land Brokerage

Land brokers deal in land for farming and the purchase of land near cities for residential, commercial, and industrial expansion. Success as a land broker depends on how accurately the income potential of the property can be determined. Farm brokers need a good working knowledge of various factors that determine a farm's capacity to produce, including agricultural knowledge and information such as market centers and transportation facilities.

Real Estate Appraising

Real estate appraisers are necessary for buyers to obtain an unbiased estimate of a property's market or commercial value. Appraisers usually work for banks or appraiser firms, and they will normally value properties by finding comparable sales in an area or by estimating the discounted value of cash flows expected from a property.

This profession is less cyclical than real estate brokerage because appraisers are required both for new home loans and for homes that are being refinanced, which happens historically when the real estate market is slow.

Property Management

Large real estate investors usually require professional property managers. Managers are responsible for negotiating leases, ensuring that tenants are satisfied and their rent is paid, and determining if the rents reflect market conditions.

A property manager needs good interpersonal and analytical skills, as well as a fair amount of negotiating prowess. This job is personally rewarding and allows you to really learn various real estate markets, should you wish to embark in this business on your own.

If you are interested in real estate property management, the Institute of Real Estate Management (IREM) is the trade association providing education and information for the property manager. Their training programs include the Certified Property Manager (CPM) and Accredited Residential Manager (ARM) designations.

Industrial and Office Brokerage

Industrial and office brokers specialize in developing, selling, or leasing property used for industry or manufacturing. Brokers need to be familiar with different types of industries and know how to determine and evaluate variables, such as transportation; proximity to raw materials, water, and power sources; labor availability; and local building, zoning, and tax laws. For additional information on this career, obtain information from the Society of Industrial and Office Realtors.

Getting Started in Real Estate

To succeed in a real estate career, you must gain knowledge, acquire new skills, work smarter, be more creative, and be able to manage your time well. Check out your state Real Estate Association on the Internet, where you will find much free information about pursuing a career in real estate. In addition, you should visit a local real estate office and ask for some suggestions of ways to begin a business in your state.

You can also find more information and insight into getting started in the various aspects of real estate in the "Resources" section at the end of this book.

Straight Talk from Bob

Realtors often have much closer personal contact with their clients than do other entrepreneurs. Thus, it's not a surprise that realtors often wind up giving gifts—or thinking about giving gifts—to their clients, and many of them seem quite adept at the art of gift-giving.

But most businesspeople sweat over the idea of giving business gifts to their clients, prospects, and customers. They don't know what to give. They do think they know when to give it, but they really don't. (I'll address that in a minute.) They worry about whether the gift is the right gift, how much to spend, and what the recipient will think.

I've escaped this particular trap, mainly because I like to give people little gifts. I do it for relatives … friends … neighbors … as well as prospects and clients.

My gift-giving method, which has been very successful for me, is simple: When I stumble across something really cool or neat that I think a particular person would enjoy, and it doesn't cost a fortune, I buy it, wrap it, and send it with a note. I know what each of my clients (and friends and relatives) likes, because I have a good memory for that sort of thing.

But you don't need a near-photographic memory to remember what people like: Just make a note in your database or address book in their record or listing.

The best business gifts relate to the other person's major interests, hobbies, and activities. I find these things out mainly by talking to them: We usually start business conferences with an exchange of pleasantries, and I ask questions so that I learn what they like. (I do this not for gift-giving purposes, but because I am genuinely interested. It also helps us find common ground, which is a great way to build relationships.)

The traditional approach to giving business gifts is to send a gift during the holiday season. The problem with doing so is twofold. First, your gift gets lost in the pile of other gifts that the prospect may receive from all her other vendors.

Second, it creates an instant expectation in the prospect that she will receive a gift from you every year. Therefore, if you skip a year, she will feel cheated. You become "stuck" having to give all those gifts to all those customers year after year.

That's why I give business gifts spontaneously—when I come across the perfect item I know a specific client would love—and not according to any schedule or annual milestone, such as a birthday or holiday.

Do not make the gift too lavish, lest it be perceived as a bribe rather than a gift. Business gifts do not have to be expensive to be appreciated. In fact, people enjoy small gifts, even little ad specialties, that bring a smile to their face.

One of my favorite gifts to give clients and prospects is an autographed copy of one of my books, and the one occasion where I do deliberately time a gift is to say "thank you" for a favor.

For instance, when I have a new book published, my joint venture partners are kind enough to promote it to their lists. When they do, I send them a short note, an autographed copy of the book, and a small Starbucks gift card.

I wish I could say they appreciate the book more than the coffee—but I suspect it is often the opposite.

10

Launching Your New Business

No matter what business you have decided to set up, you will need to take some steps to make sure you can get off to a good start. These steps apply whether your are 25, 50, or 75; if you want to succeed in a home business, you must take the time to do it right. In this chapter, you will learn about some of the steps you need to take to get your new venture up and running. We will look at:

- Choosing a legal form for your business
- Choosing and registering a business name
- Creating a business plan
- Making the necessary financial plans
- Creating a website
- Announcing your new business

Choosing a Form

First, consider how you want to set up your company. Do you wish to set it up as a sole proprietorship (only you) or do you want to incorporate the business? Corporation types include S and C corporations, limited partnerships, and limited liability corporations (LLC). Each has different financial, tax, and legal ramifications and requirements.

You must make your decision based on what services you plan to provide and what liabilities you might incur during the course of doing business. Are you in a business that is at high risk of being sued? Are

Word to the Wise

Depending on the type of business you are opening, I recommend hiring an attorney and CPA on a monthly retainer to make sure everything goes correctly right from the start. Your attorney can help set up basic contracts to use for future clients and review any contracts clients want you to sign. A CPA can help you prepare your taxes and make sure that you take advantage of laws and deductions that benefit small businesses.

clients coming to your home to do business? You'll need to be protected from anything that could occur on the premises, however obscure.

My suggestion here is to find a really good CPA (certified public accountant) and/or a lawyer in your state to look over what you plan to do and help you set everything up fully and correctly. Your choice will affect your business liabilities, personal liabilities, and how you protect your assets. You definitely want to get this step right.

You should also obtain a federal tax identification number that you will use for all your business income and expenses, as well as for any contract workers you might hire for your business and projects. Bring the paperwork sent to you when you signed up for the ID number when you register your company in your county, state, or province. Your CPA and lawyer will be able to advise you of current best practices so you don't run into trouble with the Internal Revenue Service at a later date.

Choosing a Name

Your best bet when it comes to naming your business is to use something that represents your type of business and is easy to remember. It can be as simple as operating under your own name as a corporation or sole proprietorship. Or, you can come up with a more elaborate name that reflects your business niche but does not include your name.

If marketing and public relations are not your game, think about hiring a consultant who can help you decide on a name, design a logo, and develop a slogan that represents the kind of service you want to offer your customers. If your marketing consultant is a copywriter, have him or her write copy for your website and any other promotional documents you need for advertising, marketing, and public relations.

Before you file the necessary paperwork with your new business name, you need to check to see whether that name is being used somewhere else. Contact your local, county, and state agencies or do an online search. You can find a good resource for name searches and business filing requirements broken down by state at www.usa.gov. Certain businesses, depending on the type and scope of their services, may also need to search federal registries and may need trademark or copyright protection.

Most individuals starting a new business choose to form sole LLCs or file for a "DBA" certificate, which means "doing business as." In most states, you will have to file an application with the Department of State, Division of Corporations and/or your local County Clerk's office. Depending on the nature of your business and its legal structure, you may have to meet additional licensing requirements, obtain permits, and file tax registrations before conducting business.

Creating a Business Plan

While you are wading through all of the legal decisions and paperwork, spend some time creating a business plan, which will come in really handy for a number of reasons. First, it helps you organize your business arrangements and focuses you on what needs to be done next in your organizational process. Also, if you go to a bank to open up a checking account or to seek a loan for your business, the loan officer or bank agent is going to want to know if you have such a plan, because a solid business plan allows them to see how serious you are about building your business. You may also need this documentation if you apply for grants through various foundations or for loans from the Small Business Administration (SBA).

Haven't a clue what a business plan is? Check at your local bookstore or at Amazon.com to find books that provide business plan outlines and supply sample business plans. If funds are tight, go to your local library and ask for help in finding some of these books. A good starter book would be *Business Plans Kit for Dummies*, 3rd ed., by Steven Peterson, Peter Jaret, and Barbara Schenck (For Dummies, 2010).

Taking Care of your Money

You've got a good idea of what you want to do, or maybe several ideas. Now, how do you plan to handle your finances? Do you have a business bank account set up to take in the money you receive as a freelancer?

Your account should be one that takes in all payments made by checks and any possible bank-to-bank transfers.

To save yourself a lot of time and aggravation, you should call ahead to the banks you are considering using and ask to speak to the person who handles business accounts. Interview several banks to determine the one that offers the best services for the lowest fees. Start with the bank where your personal accounts are held, especially if you are looking for a business loan, since they already know you.

Often, the bank's nominal monthly maintenance fees will be waived if you satisfy certain conditions, like maintaining a certain balance in the account or paying a certain minimum number of monthly expenses from the account. Even if you don't satisfy those requirements, ask for the waiver of the fee.

Tell the business manager what type of entity you have formed, and he will tell you what documentation you need to bring with you to set up the account. Typically, you will need your driver's license or other official photo identification, the tax identification number for the business, a copy of your articles of incorporation or operating agreement, Department of State filing receipt, and the stock or member's certificate issued to you, indicating your ownership interest in the business.

Open a business checking account and get a business debit or credit card. You can also set up a merchant account for credit card purchases, if that is applicable to your business. Now, you're in business!

You can also create a PayPal business account online, which is an easy way to get paid efficiently and quickly through e-mail invoicing. PayPal allows your clients to pay with credit cards, even if you haven't set up a merchant account. There is a small percentage charge for the PayPal service, but that fee may be deductible as a business expense at the end of the year. Just keep careful records of everything you do financially. Get every dollar back in tax deductions that you can.

Establishing Financial Goals

It is also vitally important for you to establish your financial goals. For instance, let's say you decide you want to take in $200,000 in revenue the first year, a good goal to begin with. Now, you need to drill down and figure out what you plan to make per month to reach that goal. Drill down further and look at your weekly goals, too. You will have to figure out what you need to charge for products or services in order to reach

HOW BOB DOES IT

When I started freelancing in 1982, every client paid by check. Now, they pay by check, wire transfer, credit card, and PayPal. The advantage of taking credit cards and PayPal is that it allows you to get your retainer immediately in order to lock in a job before something happens to change the client's mind.

that year-end goal of $200,000. Sit down with your calculator and start dividing by hours and weeks to work out your income goals.

So, there are 52 weeks in the year, but you want to take out eight weeks for vacation time during the summer. That leaves you with 44 weeks to make $200,000. That amount divided by 44 equals $4,545.45 per week. Dividing that by five days will equal $909.10 per day. If you work eight hours per day, that will equal $113.64 an hour.

The next part of your financial outline is determining what it will cost per year to run the business. This is your balance sheet for the business; what is left over is what you or your company has made for the year as profit. The expenses include office supplies, business supplies, utilities and rent, payments to vendors and contract workers, and finally payments to yourself. Always be sure to pay yourself.

Of particular importance for those of us over 50 is making sure we are putting money away quarterly or yearly, preferably into retirement funds that earn the best interest we can find. Your CPA or money manager will be able to advise you on how to protect your money and make it work for you.

SETTING UP A WEBSITE

No matter what kind of business you have, you must create a website. If you're over 50, you may not really recognize how indispensable a web presence is to a business today, but skipping this step will limit your chances in a world where few people under 30 have ever used the Yellow Pages and believe that if a piece of information is worth knowing, a Google search will find it. In addition, a website opens your business up to the world outside your local neighborhood. With a website, many businesses can be run entirely from home, and your website will work for you 24/7. So, having a business website is indispensable, whether you sell products or provide services.

How much time you spend creating your website and how detailed it needs to be will depend largely on what kind of business you are establishing. A simple one-page site with business details and contact information might be all you need for an import/export business. If you are a freelancer specializing in writing or design, your website should be more elaborate and provide a showcase of your talents. If you are selling items online, you will need to provide photos, add a shopping cart, and indicate ways for customers to pay for their purchases.

Acquiring a Domain Name

To set up a website, you first need a domain name. That's the part of a web address that comes after the www. There are many online services that will register a domain name, including the popular www.GoDaddy.com and www.UltraCheapDomains.com. This step is very easy to do, even if you have limited computer knowledge, and the fees can be as low as about $10 per year.

Just log on to one of the services and search for a particular domain name of your choice to see if it is in use. The ideal domain name should be easy to remember and easy to relate to your business name. You may want to start by entering the name of your business as a domain name. Most businesses register as a ".com." If your first choice of domain name is not available, you may be able to make it work with only a slight revision, such as adding a word like "the" or "best" before it, or "store," "online," or "shop" after it.

At most of the domain registration services, you can acquire a domain name and have a website up and running in a few hours, using easy-to-use templates from the site. Or, you can pay a bit more and have the service set it all up for you, including adding your company logo. These services even offer very reasonable hosting plans for your website, which you will need for your site to be "live" and accessible to the world.

Creating a Website

Sound scary to do all this by yourself? Well, it really isn't anymore. There are so many services that will walk you through the setup, step-by-step, or supply you with templates to get the look you need and the features you want. Or, you can hire someone to set up and/or keep your website updated. If money is tight, you can look for a college student or recent

HOW BOB DOES IT

When I was creating my initial website, I took my last name for my domain name because it is short, easy to remember, and identifies me: www.bly.com.

For other sites, I always try to select domain names that are easy to remember. For example, for my site selling my e-book *How to Write and Sell E-Books,* I set up a website with domain name: www.MyVeryFirstEbook.com.

college grad who would be willing to set you up for a reduced price in order to get a sample for her portfolio. Or, look on Craigslist or fiver.com.

Once your website is up and running, you can also sign up for an e-mail with your website address, which looks very professional. If you have accounts at social media sites like Facebook and Twitter, you can add buttons which will allow clients to go to your social media sites straight from your business website. And, on your social media sites, you should have your website links in full view so that people who find you there can go directly to your website and learn about your products and services.

MAKING YOUR WEBSITE MORE VISIBLE

Once you have created a website, how do you make sure anyone sees it? The best way is to add meta tags in the coding of your web pages and also write copy content that contains words search engines can pick up during a search. Known as SEO (search engine optimization), it does take some time and testing to find out what will bring you the best results. The objective is to use keywords that will move your page as close as possible to the top of a list generated by a user's search request. The title of your web page should reflect words in your content, and your words, especially keywords, should reflect the purpose of your website and its existence.

There are multiple books and websites written about how to conduct SEO. If you're confused by the very concept, a good place to start to educate yourself is www.RocketFace.com, which includes tutorials on all aspects of website design. Or, for more information, search online for "website optimization" and "how to optimize a website."

Announcing Your New Business to Your Community

It's time to get your new business noticed!

If you want to get the attention of your community, you should submit a press release to the local media. A press release is generally a written announcement to the media regarding the launch of a business, a new product or development, an event, or a significant change in supervisory personnel. Basically, anything newsworthy and of interest to the public would qualify.

You can prepare and submit your own press release using online resources, or you can hire a copywriter to create one for you. Some online services will handle both preparation and submission of the press release for varying fees. If distributed broadly, it could be seen by local as well as national and worldwide audiences online and could generate both increased sales and traffic to your website. Although there is no guarantee that a press release will get "picked up" (or printed) by any media outlet, be mindful to maintain a "newsy" tone because copy that reads like a company advertisement will almost certainly be rejected.

An often overlooked, but very effective, tool for targeted marketing is the professional magazine, or trade magazine. These journals are specifically tailored to appeal to a narrow, targeted audience interested in a particular trade or industry.

Commonly filled with advertisements and job postings for the industry, a trade magazine is the perfect place for a business owner to publish an article of interest to his particular target audience. These publications are not read by the general public, but rather by the kind of people most likely to hire you. Just being published in a trade publication lends a sense of credibility to your business.

Be sure to check out *Bacon's Newspaper and Magazine Directory* for the most up-to-date contact information at each trade magazine and newspaper.

Signs of Life

If you have a home-based business that serves your community, you can advertise through local billboards, local publication ads, and anywhere else you can imagine putting your mark—or sign. Obviously, if you live in a residential area, no signage will be allowed for your business, but you might be able to rent a sign for your business at the shopping strip a mile away.

Depending on the type of business you have, you can paint your signage on your truck or car, which can provide you a lot of "mileage" in your local advertising. You can also use magnetic vehicle signs that can easily be taken on or off as desired. Check online for "signage" to find both types of car ads.

BUSINESS CARDS AND LETTERHEADS

Planning to send out marketing packets and business letters to potential clients? Use your company logo on your business cards and letterheads. Start out with a small packet of business cards until you see how many you use over a period of time. Then order more. Decide if you want to include an address or if you wish to use only your phone number, website address, and e-mail address. You should also include a USP statement on your business card. A USP—unique selling proposition—is a statement about what your business does for your client.

You should design your own logo—or hire someone to design it for you—and add it to your business card, letterhead, and website. Make it unique, something your potential clients will remember every time they see it. This use of your logo is a type of branding for your business, so that your clients will remember the logo and what it stands for. If you create your own business cards and stationery, you can save the designs onto a CD or flash drive to take with you to a print shop so they can easily transfer it to their computer and print your items.

Don't try to do the printing yourself unless you use really good paper and a very high-end printer. Resolutions for colors and type should be perfect. The last thing you want to do is present yourself as an amateur. This is not an area to scrimp.

ATTENTION-GETTING METHODS

An asphalt company once got my attention by throwing onto my neglected driveway a baggie full of broken blacktop bits with their flier inside. Simple. Clever. Effective. But you don't have to throw rocks at the neighbors to get your business noticed.

There are other tried-and-true methods, such as talking over the fence or at the neighborhood coffee shop, or distributing fliers at the supermarket and public library, or buying very cheap ads in the local shopper that people receive for free by mail. Never underestimate the power of a small, cheap ad in a program for your local high school basketball team or in a church or temple bulletin.

Offer to do a presentation at the library! It's free publicity for your business and will help establish you as a credible expert in your field. You can do the same for other local groups, like homemakers or seniors. To promote your business, be sure to bring business cards and free booklets—if you have them—and a sheet for attendees to sign up for your e-mail newsletter or e-mail list.

You need to network. Join your local Chamber of Commerce and other business-related community organizations, such as the Rotary Club or Knights of Columbus. Your new bank manager may also set you up with a local networking group, or you can check your local paper's business section for other local networking groups and join one in your area.

Friends and Family

Share the good news with your friends, family, and acquaintances! These are the folks who are already "sold" on you and want to see you succeed. You don't have to convince them to use your business; you just have to let them know about it. But if you stop there, you're doing yourself a disservice. You need to ask them to refer your new business to *their* friends, family, and acquaintances!

Finally, you're ready to employ the less personal—though very effective—methods of announcing your new business. There are bulk e-mail notices you can send to your address book on your own or through a service such as Constant Contact. Just be careful not to spam anyone when sending e-mails. You can also send out a direct-mail postcard announcement. These postcards can be ordered from online sources, a local printer, or created by you through some of the "Office Suite" business software programs.

Word to the Wise

For some of your friends and relatives, anything less than a phone call announcing your new business would be an insult. So, first determine who, besides Mom and Aunt Betty, needs your personal attention, and then make those calls. Next, figure out who needs a handwritten note, as opposed to an e-mail or postcard, and get those cards in the mail.

A very effective and inexpensive way to announce your new business is through social media outlets such as Facebook, Twitter, LinkedIn, and Foursquare, to name a few.

Create a "Local Business" Facebook page for your new business and ask all your personal Facebook friends to "Like" your business page. Use Twitter to tweet about your new business. If you are a professional, LinkedIn is a must to let your colleagues know about your venture!

YELLOW PAGES LISTINGS

If you're old enough to be reading this book, you remember when the phone book was one of the most important books in the house. Yellow Pages and residential/business phone books are still delivered to our homes, but few households rely on them much any more because all the information can now be found online. However, if your business is based heavily on local clients, it is crucial to get listed in both versions. If you have a service business, you may just need an online Yellow Pages listing, which can be accessed from anywhere in the world.

You can search online by using the term "Yellow Pages" and see what's involved in obtaining an online listing and, perhaps, an advertisement. Ask a local advertising consultant about different pricing in your area if you want to be included only in the print version.

STRAIGHT TALK FROM BOB

People frequently ask me, "What are your top five strategies for getting clients?" Here's what I like to tell them:

1. Create a content-rich website describing your services. Then load it up with free content. The content positions you as an expert in your field. And, it gets visitors to spend a lot of time on your site. I have dozens of free articles and free special reports posted on my site: www.bly.com/newsite/Pages/articles.php.
2. SEO (search-engine optimization). Optimize your website for search engines using keywords related to your service. This will bring a lot of traffic to your site. Have a form on the site where visitors can register and tell you about their needs. This will convert traffic into sales leads. See my example at www.bly.com/contact.

3. Start an e-newsletter. Write and publish a monthly online newsletter. Create a sign-up page and drive traffic to it using e-mail marketing, Google AdWords, and other traffic generation methods. Work to build your subscriber list from hundreds to thousands. The more prospects who see your newsletter, the better known you become.
4. Write articles. Writing and publishing how-to articles on your specialty further positions you as an expert in your field. You can post the published articles on your website to add content and impress visitors. You can also use article reprints as mailers. For more information on how to write articles for both print magazines and online newsletters, check out: www.GetFamousWritingArticles.com.
5. Give talks. Find local chapters of associations to which your prospects belong. Offer to give a talk at a lunch or dinner meeting. Since these local chapters don't pay speakers, they are always looking for someone to give a presentation for free. Volunteer to do it. If you give a good talk, some prospects in the audience will become interested in hiring you. Offer a free article reprint or tip sheet in exchange for their business cards. Then follow up by e-mail or phone.

And, a bonus tip: Record your speech. Duplicate the talk on audio CDs and mail these with your brochure to prospects who request information on your services. Post the audio as an mp3 file on your website and send your e-newsletter subscribers a link where they can hear it. If you want to avoid travel or are nervous about speaking live before a group, give and record an audio teleconference on your topic. Invite your online subscribers to attend for free. Post-conference, make the audio recording available as an mp3 and CD.

11

Setting Up Your Home Office

Configuring and furnishing your office can be one of the most enjoyable parts of setting up your business at home. However, there are numerous factors to consider before you make final decisions and purchases, so take some time to think about what will work best in your home and with the type of business you plan to establish.

Having the right furniture, lighting, computers, printers, fax machine, copy machine, and any other hardware you need for accomplishing the job makes it much more comfortable when you sit down to go to work. From my experience, having all the tools you'll need to run your business efficiently in one handy place is a major part of being successful.

If you are lucky enough to be building a new house as you are establishing your home business, be sure to review your blueprint plans with your project manager/contractor and decide the best location for your office before the plans are locked in. More likely, you will be converting a room or space in your existing house into your office. Either way, you need to give thought to the location and setup of the office space.

If you are planning to use a room in your main house, spend some time thinking about what kind of view you'll see out your windows; consider where the sun is during the day and how it will affect your office lighting and your computer screen placement. It's nice to look out the window, daydream, or ponder solutions, but if you have sun glare on your monitor, then window availability won't do you much good.

Consider whether your potential office is far enough away from the main hub of family life so that you will not be interrupted by barking dogs and noisy children. When you are on the phone working up a joint venture deal with a client, you do not want all three of your grandchildren to come barging in, screaming at the top of their lungs. (Of course, you could always lock your door.)

It is ideal for some to build a separate, small, garage-style office to the side of the main house so you can shut everyone and everything out of your thought and work processes. You can add a bathroom off to one side and, maybe, a kitchenette with a microwave and coffeemaker. This kind of arrangement is ideal for those who prefer to work in a more isolated setting but enjoy being able to step out the door and visit family and pets in the main house. You can have lunch with the folks, play ball with the dog, and then go back to work.

Word to the Wise

If you have a home office in your house, then you may not have to worry about zoning, unless you plan to have clients come to the house. Generally, most residential areas won't tolerate businesses in the area, so there may be some repercussions if you have clients or deliveries coming to your house on a frequent basis.

Before you build an add-on office or convert your garage into an office, you will first need to check your local zoning laws and building codes to find out if you can build behind your house. Local laws vary, and some areas have more restrictive laws than others.

Choosing the Room Style and Accessories

Once you have decided where to locate your office, it's time to think about what will go into it. You may be repurposing a room that is already full of usable furniture and all you plan to do is shuffle things around a bit to make your workspace more efficient. Or, you may be looking to completely redecorate so that the room will feel like an office instead of a teenager's bedroom or a children's playroom.

If you're going the remodel route, you get to decide what color to paint the walls, what type of flooring you feel comfortable with, whether to add in some favorite photographs or art pieces, and where to strategically place those in the room. This can be an exciting time; perhaps

How Bob Does It

I used to have a rented office outside the house. It was a 15-minute drive on local roads, so I never fought any highway traffic. I also liked driving the quarter hour to and from work. In the morning, it gave me a chance to wake up, so by the time I hit the office, I was ready to go. In the evening it allowed me to decompress before getting home.

However, when my wife was diagnosed with cancer a couple of years ago, I closed the outside office and finished our attic to build a home office. It is half a flight of steps above the second floor, so it is really high up and I have a truly beautiful view of the backyard, which is filled with trees, from a big picture window in front of my desk.

In my office, I have a black-and-white, high-speed laser printer. I also have a Brother Intellifax 2800 with a dedicated phone line, and I have another business phone line for voice separate from our home phone. Furniture is ordinary: a couple of desks, a table holding the printer and PCs, a bookcase, coffee table, couch, two office chairs.

Since I cannot afford to be without my computer for even an hour, due to constant client deadlines, I have two PCs running side-by-side with a TruLink switch. If one computer fails, I press a button and can immediately switch to the back-up computer. Both computers access the same files stored on a network storage device (NSD). If the NSD fails, the files are backed up remotely offsite.

you've spent years working in a cubicle decorated in industrial gray or in a windowless office with strict rules forbidding personal decorations or flair. Now, you get to cut loose and personalize your space the way you want.

But before you choose furniture and decorations on the basis of looks alone, spend some time thinking about how you will be using the space. You might also consider who will clean the room—if it's you and you hate to clean, use materials that are easy to maintain. (I never clean my office and instead hire a cleaning service that comes twice a month.)

You also need to be realistic about the difference between your needs now and as you grow older. You're probably already noticing that you don't see as well as you used to; as we get older, our eyes don't take in as much light as they once did, so you will need to make sure you have good overhead lighting and strategic spots for lamps. Make sure chairs provide good back and arm support and that your desks are ergonomically suited to your body.

If you have a color scheme in mind before choosing your furniture and flooring, take paint samples with you when you go to select your furniture and flooring, whether it is carpet or vinyl flooring. If you are putting in wood flooring, take a sample of the flooring when choosing your cabinet style, wood, and finish. Finding that your installed wood floor doesn't match or complement the wood finish on your cabinets can be an unpleasant surprise—and one you will have to look at day after day. Throw rugs can help diffuse any problem that might arise; just make sure the rugs complement the furniture and color scheme in the room.

Design can get complicated, but thinking ahead, planning, and doing your research before buying will save you time and lots of money. Also, don't forget to purchase a floor piece, usually made of clear hard vinyl, which can go under your chair and feet while you are sitting at your desk. It's easy to keep clean and leaves an underlying wood or vinyl floor free from shoe and chair roller scratches.

Layout Design

Before you start moving furniture, you should sketch your office layout, or you can try out free home design software by SmartDraw (seven-day free trial) at www.SmartDraw.com or SketchUp (free, upgrade available for purchase) at www.SketchUp.com. Do an Internet search for "free home design software" to find other available software programs. It's fun to virtually see your dream office before you even get started on the real thing. It may also give you a chance to catch potential layout problems before you build or buy office furniture and equipment. Once you insert your room measurements and window and door placements, you're ready to start designing.

One important aspect of your design is to decide how you expect to operate in your office on a daily basis, what needs to be close at hand, what can be stored farther away from you in the room, and the ease of using common walking paths in your office. Your design should include lighting fixture placements, access to peripherals like printers, fax/scanner machines, and copiers, and the location of electrical outlets to accommodate all your equipment. Never overload one circuit and use protected plug strips to help with multiple electronic plug-ins. Add more grounded circuits if you see that you need more available in one part of the room. You'll want to complete this electrical work before installing anything else.

If you will be in a garage office and plan to have a kitchenette and bathroom, make sure you have all the grounded circuits and plumbing you need to handle that usage. Check this before you add in flooring, cabinets, bookcases, and anything else that will get in the way of the plumbing and electrical installation.

Storage Cabinets and Bookcases

If you are going to buy ready-made cabinets to go against the walls or to create stand-alone islands, the usual standard base cabinet dimensions are 12" wide by 24" deep (the measurement from the front to the back wall). Corner cabinets are also available as lazy Susans or blind corners, where two base cabinets meet at a 90-degree angle and half of one is covered up by the other. If you plan to be in your office for several years, consider going with upgraded products.

You will also need to install a countertop, as these cabinets have open tops. The cabinets are made to accept any kind of countertop, preferably laminates, which now come in some really beautiful colors.

The cheapest option might be the "grab and go" cabinets that come raw, but ready to be painted and finished. Other in-store cabinet lines have several finishes already applied, but will cost a bit more. You can have your home improvement store install your cabinets, but it usually requires a professional measurement first. Be aware that ready-made cabinets are, for the most part, constructed from particle board, with wood doors. These cabinets are actually designed for kitchens, but they work quite well for basic office storage.

If you need ready-made bookshelves, check out raw furniture companies online to view products and prices. Websites such as www.UnfinishedFurnitureExpo.com and www.1UnfinishedFurniture.com give you an idea of what's offered. You can also do a keyword search for "unfinished wood furniture." Or, if you're handy, build your own.

Color Schemes and Decoration

A great way to decide on paint color for your office is to check out samples at a home improvement center. You can take these samples home and hold up different colors to the wall, or even hold up several color combinations. Choose something that you'll love to look at on a daily basis, something that will work with your lighting conditions, and that makes you feel good and ready to work whenever you come into the room. You will be spending a lot of time in this room, so it's important to be comfortable and happy. Again, don't forget to check these samples against flooring and cabinet samples, too.

When designing your office, you need to consider if you will have clients coming by or if this room will be solely for your personal use. If you have clients coming in often, you'll want to develop a more professional look. If it is just for you, you might prefer to give a more casual look to the layout and furnishings.

Office Furniture and Supplies

Invest in a really good desk and a swivel, padded office chair. You must feel comfortable, because you'll probably spend many hours sitting and working at your desk. Would you like a curved desk or a rectangular desk? Do you prefer curved glass or a nice wood top? Your choice of desk and office chair will depend on your taste and also the convenience for accessing your tools of the trade. A nice curved desk with drawers on either side allows you to sit in the middle,directly in front of your laptop, and to reach to either side for papers and books you've placed there for your project.

You can also place bookcases behind your chair in a corner of the room, maybe two on either wall, meeting at the corner. All your reference and trade materials, books, DVDs, and CDs, can be stashed right there, reachable with just the swivel of your chair. On one side of the end of the bookcases could be a stand for your printer and your fax machine, or a combination printer/fax/scanner/phone.

If you've decided to get special-order cabinets for your office, you can also purchase similar style bookcases and desks in the same brand. If you are adding raw wood furniture and plan to paint or stain everything but can't find specific pieces—except in the special order brand books—have your design consultant check to see if the brand also offers unfinished versions of what they show in the books.

Before setting up your office, make sure you have more than enough drawers, filing cabinets, and working surfaces for the needs of your profession. Think ahead about the need for storage expansions. If you do drafting work, maybe you want more than one or two tables set up, so you can move from one project to another without having to move things around. Make it easy and fun to work in your office, so you are always happy to be there.

Word to the Wise

Make a habit of leaving your work in your office when you are done for the day. If you have a family and pets, they will want some of your time. It is also good for you to move away from your work, wipe away the work cobwebs and dramas, have some fun, eat meals with your family, and maintain family and friend relationships, while talking about everything but work.

Leaving your work in your office can also help you stay organized, because papers, books, and flash drives can get misplaced or lost if you carry them outside of the office, which is (hopefully) organized with a place for all your material. Misplaced materials can turn into a big disaster and cause added stress that you don't need.

No, it's not fun when you find out Fido chewed the USB flash drive to your latest project. Well, it did look like a bone, didn't it?

Computers for Your Office, Your Life

Once you have settled on the design, layout, and basic furniture for your home office, you need to consider what you will put in the office so that you can work. And, no matter what type of business you are establishing, you will need a computer—or several computers.

If you've never really bought a computer but just relied on the one supplied to you by your employer, you may find yourself overwhelmed by the choices and the terminology. Take the time to do your homework; read reviews from technology gurus and ask people you know what kind of computer they use and enjoy. And, be sure to carefully consider how you will be using your computer in your new business.

Laptop vs. Desktop

Your first decision will likely be whether to buy a laptop or a desktop computer—or if you want to invest in both. Laptops allow you to carry your office with you. If you have an Internet access plan and connection device for your laptop, you can basically run your business while away from home. If you have a home office, however, you may want to also invest in a desktop tower, which remains stationary in a cabinet or on the floor, along with a good-sized flat screen monitor (between 21" to 31" wide) and a wireless keyboard and mouse. Your laptop can wait patiently on the side until needed, such as when you want to go sit out in the garden or visit a coffee shop at a bookstore. You can transfer your documents from the desktop to the laptop by way of a flash drive or through Cloud storage and head on out.

If and when you need to travel, the laptop is obviously the best way to go, but do invest in a well-padded, sturdy carrying case that has plenty of sections for notepads, pens, cords and cables, CDs, USB sticks, external hard drive for storage, and whatever else you need. Depending on your business, you might want to invest in a portable printer so you can print information for a client to review or sign during a meeting when you are nowhere near a printer.

The stationary desktop in your home office is usually a more robust system than a laptop, and, at the least, it should serve as a great backup to your laptop in case it goes down. Or vice versa. It really depends on what you need to do on a computer. If you are a graphics designer or video game designer, chances are you'll want to go with a tower. If you are creating documents with limited graphics, the laptop may be the better way to go. You can purchase a PC that uses the latest Windows platform or a MacBook using Apple's Mac OS platform, which is normally preferred by those working in graphics, photography, and other graphic-heavy design professions.

Desktop hard drives, as well as portable external hard drives for backups, can come as large as 1 to 2 TBs (terabytes). A middle-of-the-road usage Intel Quad Core processor will handle online video games, heavy graphics, photographs, and other multimedia. The best way to decide what you want to purchase or upgrade to is to review weekly sales ads from retailers such as BestBuy and Fry's Electronics.

Check out sizes of monitors to find a screen large enough to meet your needs. Make things easy on your aging eyes if you do a lot of work on the computer. Ask a store assistant to provide information on video graphics size and memory, based on the computer you are buying. If your computer comes with an HDMI plug, you can even choose a TV flat screen with an HDMI outlet as a hook up. (If you like to watch Netflix and your laptop has an HDMI plug, you can plug it into your HDMI television, download streaming movies and shows, and watch what you want. Just make sure you have the appropriate cables for hooking up your two components.)

Finally, your desktop tower usually comes with a basic keyboard and plug-in mouse. That may be fine for your purposes, but you may prefer wireless keyboards and mouse systems, which provide more ergonomic benefits for typing and mouse-clicks because you don't have to worry about cords and you can position the units wherever you want.

Choose a printer capable of printing your documents as professionally as possible. If you have color photographs, you'll want a photo-capable printer that captures color hues and tones as accurately as possible. Most of these are fairly expensive, but it is better to invest in the best equipment possible when starting your business, as the quality of your presentations and other graphics will allow clients to view you as a professional, inspiring their confidence. If printing documents is not a big issue, maybe a printer/scanner/fax/phone combination may be your best bet.

Internet Connection

Being able to connect to the Internet is the greatest factor in allowing you to work from home. So, do your homework and find out what various providers in your area can offer in terms of speed, reliability, and portability.

More and more companies are getting into the game of providing Internet access, especially in supposed cost-saving packages that also include dish/broadband/DSL access television service and phone service. Thoroughly investigate each provider for Internet speed, offerings in TV channels based on what you'll actually use, and whether you think you really need a home phone service.

Some of the most popular providers currently are Time Warner Cable, AT&T, and DirectTV. Research each service in your area for package deals, based on what your particular needs are. If you don't watch television much and can access what you like to watch on your computer, then just get Internet access.

If your Internet provider allows you to add a portable hotspot service, you can log on through your laptop at just about any place where there is an accessible tower with whom your service provider has a contract agreement with. Sometimes, you will find that your portable hotspot won't work 30 miles away from home, yet at other times you can travel halfway across the country and have access. The unpredictability can be annoying sometimes, but you just have to check accessibility by zip code on the Internet before you travel out of town. Log into your service account and find the link that shows your service coverage map.

Another way you can get Internet access is to find out if your cell phone service has tethering capabilities to hook up to your laptop. This is a fairly new arrangement on the market and not all services or all phone types carry this ability yet. If you haven't bought a new phone in the past three years, you might want to upgrade. So, this would be the time to find out which phones and services provide tethering between your phone and laptop. Once tethered, your laptop works off of the phone service access to the Internet. Before you try this, you need to know if your phone service plan limits the amount of gigabyte transfers of information per month, as some services are now cutting back on usage amounts.

Business Software

A common mistake new business owners make is trying to personally handle every aspect of the business, including all the administrative jobs. They get buried under the paperwork, never get off the phone, and don't have time left to actually provide the services or ship the product—much less do any networking or marketing. It's a road map to burnout and failure.

The purpose of business software is to increase profits, decrease costs, and speed production. It helps your computer automate the jobs often held by one or more employees, thereby saving you money in salary and benefits, or in outsourcing the work. All business owners can benefit from some level of software to streamline their business and alleviate the time-sucking burden of managing the many jobs on their own.

At a minimum, business computers need antivirus, spyware, and firewall protection. A popular software choice which covers all three areas of concern is McAfee Antivirus Plus, which is just one of many equally good available products.

In addition, most businesses will need an Office Suite software program, which generally contains several essential integrated programs, such as word processing, e-mail and contact management, data-processing, spreadsheets, and more. A popular example of such a comprehensive package is Microsoft Office Professional.

Most businesses also use an accounting software program, such as Intuit QuickBooks Pro, to manage payroll, tax collection and reporting, produce financial reports, and simplify data entry.

As an option to purchasing software that takes up space in your computer, you can use a "cloud-based" business management program to do many of the same tasks. One user-friendly option is Google Apps for Business, which offers a 30-day free trial. Some of its features include business e-mail management, and calendar and contact management.

One of the benefits of this type of "cloud-based" program is that it is web-based and is therefore accessible to you from any computer or device, including mobile phones. You don't have to be at the home base to use it. Also, it doesn't require any hardware or software, and it requires minimal administration—so you don't need to be, or to hire, an IT specialist to maintain it.

There are also countless applications, called "apps," which you can add to these cloud-based programs to customize the software to your particular business needs. Many of these apps are free or nominally priced, and they include accounting, finance, document management, and inventory programs, to name a few.

Computerizing Accounts Payable and Receivable

Even if you are able to get by initially with a primitive "system" like a shoe box of receipts or a two-accordion file system for your accounts payable and accounts receivable, you will need something more sophisticated as your business grows. This is true whether you sell products or provide services.

As discussed in the prior section, you can manage your accounts receivable and accounts payable through a business software package like Intuit QuickBooks Pro or through apps added to cloud-based business management tools. Your local office supply chain store usually has knowledgeable employees to help you choose an accounting software system best suited to your business.

As a business owner, you may need to hire a CPA to prepare your business tax return. In addition to consulting with your CPA prior to choosing which type of business entity to form for tax purposes, he or she will likely be happy to recommend a computerized accounting system for your business. After all, your CPA will be using those records to prepare your tax return.

And, speaking of tax returns, you need to keep records and receipts for all the office supplies and furnishings you buy and all the modifications you make to create your home office—and expenses you encounter in running your office. Office furniture, expenses tied to remodeling or building your home office, supplies, and equipment MAY apply to your tax deductions—talk to your CPA about these.

A good CPA who is familiar with home-based businesses, business structures, and how taxes relate to each one can be invaluable and can help you handle the quarterly tax payments (due in January, April, June, and September) that you must make for federal and state estimations.

Organization

Keeping receipts for your CPA is just one small part of the organization you will need to succeed in your new home-based business. Implementing a good organization plan for your physical office and the files and programs in your computer is crucial. You want to have a place to put all your files, an easy-to-find paper and electronic filing system arrangement, and a place to sit comfortably while you do your work. Have your tradebooks and magazines handy, so you have information at your fingertips whenever you need it.

Perhaps you want to set up your computer organization system in a way that mirrors your physical files—you can use the same labels and subheadings, maybe even use similar color codes. There are many ways to organize your physical and virtual files, but you need to choose a system that makes sense for you and the way you work. You don't want to spend hours every week searching for a piece of paper or a digital file that you need to finish a project.

Computer Filing

There is information to be found on the Internet about almost any subject. But when working on a project, you need to be careful to label information you find so that you can find it again for future reference. And always be sure to save the website link. That information should go inside a folder on your computer that holds your current project notes,

How Bob Does It

My youngest son, a computer major at Carnegie Mellon, doesn't believe in paper and keeps all his files electronic. I am the opposite, and so my home office has 10 metal, four-drawer file cabinets with hanging Pendaflex files.

Files are organized the usual way, alphabetically, but with two cabinets for client files, one for my online business, and others holding copywriting samples and other documents.

other references, your actual product report, and anything else connected to that project.

You can also copy any research into a larger folder for all research done over a particular period of your business. That makes it easier should you need to find information you read some time ago but can't remember which project folder it originally went into.

Organize your main electronic business folder in such a way that you can find anything you need in one directory whenever you need immediate access. Your main folder can be called MY OFFICE. From there, build subdirectories with titles like INVOICES. In this folder, you can separate out invoices for CLIENTS and VENDORS, and you can drill down from there.

Back to your main directory: You can create a file called MARKETING. Inside that file, create a folder for CLIENTS. Inside the CLIENTS folder, create a separate folder for each client by name that will hold all folders for different projects you do for that client.

If you have all your folders organized according to your projects, and by clients, then you should have no trouble keeping up with where you filed your documents.

Straight Talk From Bob

Let me share a little tip I use to stay productive in my business without getting bored or burned out.

It's a variation of the famous Pareto 80/20 principle, which says that 80 percent of your results come from 20 percent of your efforts.

Example: In Internet marketing, 80 percent of your online income will come from 20 percent of your e-list subscribers. If you test 10 Google pay-per-click ads, 80 percent of the clicks will be generated by 2 of the ads.

In my freelance writing, I use the Pareto Principle this way: 80 percent of assignments I take are in areas where I already have experience and expertise, and 20 percent of my writing is in areas that are new to me.

Why this 80/20 ratio?

By spending 80 percent of my time (in reality, my ratio is actually closer to 90/10) in familiar areas, I can work much faster because of my knowledge and experience. So my productivity soars.

By spending 10 percent to 20 percent of my time working in new areas, I stay fresh and prevent boredom from setting in.

I have come across several writers who tell me they abhor specialization and always write articles on new topics their editors assign them. In this way, they are never bored.

On the other hand, they don't amortize what they learn on one topic over other assignments. So, all that learning is in essence wasted, at least from a work perspective. These generalists have to learn a new subject for every assignment. As a result, each new article takes a long time, and their output and income are limited as a result.

At the opposite end of the spectrum, I read one writer who seems to spend 100 percent of his time writing about an exceedingly narrow niche: silver prices.

I admire the authority with which he writes on this subject. Indeed, he is likely one of the foremost experts in the world on silver.

On the other hand, if I wrote about nothing but silver prices 40 to 60 hours a week, every week of the year, I'd be bored to tears.

I can't tell you what to do or how to spend your time at work. But I do recommend the Pareto Principle: Spend 80 percent of your time on familiar tasks and 20 percent of your time exploring new areas.

This strategy keeps me productive, fresh, and engaged. Maybe it can do the same for you, too.

12

Marketing and Promoting Your New Business

As a new business owner, you can't sit back and wait for the phone to ring; you have to *make* it ring. There are multiple channels out there to let people know that you are open for business, including some you may have never considered. Spend a little time developing a marketing plan, thinking about how you can use various channels to generate sales leads that turn into contracts, clients, and revenue. This chapter will give you brief glimpses into a number of channels you might consider utilizing, including:

- Web marketing
- Online advertising
- E-mail marketing
- Social media
- Direct mail
- Print advertising
- Sales brochures
- Cold calling
- Telemarketing
- Referral marketing system

Marketing Plan

Hand in hand with your business plan is your marketing plan, which describes how you intend to bring in customers and money to make your business successful. Marketing includes—but is not limited to—paid advertising, although that might be a key facet of your plan. Marketing also includes what is usually called public relations—how you develop a good public image for your business through social media and other means. Advertising and public relations should work hand in hand, and you can use many of the same channels, such as social media and print publications to develop both.

To create your marketing plan, you need to conduct research in a number of areas, such as competition, potential clients for your new client database, finding where and how to promote yourself to the best advantage, advertising, public relations, social media, website creation and hosting, your logo, and a host of other aspects connected with marketing. You may want to read my book *The Marketing Plan Handbook*, published in 2010 by Entrepreneur Press, for more details about each of these specific areas.

Your marketing plan will outline how you plan to check out the competition, what it is they do, and how successful they are at it. This is more in the line of market research and can become quite involved. However, the more you know what others are doing, the more knowledgeable you are about your own services and how to focus them on your own clients.

Knowing who else is out there offering the same services or products as you is very important to the foundation of your marketing plan. Essentially, what you can learn from a competitor is found in their marketing materials online or through packets sent out to interested customers. Get on mailing lists to see what competitors are doing, information which will help you immensely in figuring out how to make your offer or product better. Sign up for newsletters, too, to keep up with all the current news.

Your age and experience can provide a big boost for you in this area. You may have decades of experience in the field you are entering as a business owner; if so, you already know a lot about your competition. In fact, you may be planning to compete against your former employer and you may know exactly how you plan to do that.

But what if you are looking to enter a new field or set up shop in a new area? The best way to get information quickly is through the Internet. If you don't really know how to do Internet research, visit my site www.FastOnlineResearch.com to get started. The skills this site offers are well worth the money and time you will spend to add this tool to your skill set.

Word to the Wise

What if you don't really have the time or desire to do background research? Then search online for Internet research specialists and market research analysts; you can hire someone to provide you the information you need to produce a detailed marketing plan. The specialist will collect articles and other documentation for you and usually charges by the hour. Pricing will vary according to the niche you are in and difficulty of research. The key is that this kind of assistance can save you a lot of time, which you can devote to another key project issue that does require your sole attention.

Advertising

Your marketing plan should address several areas, and advertising is key. Methods of advertising your business can include billboards, ads in newspapers and magazines, online ads and banners, social media, and virtual advertising. Research done in advance to determine how your competitors are advertising is very important here, as is obtaining pricing for various types of ads and figuring out how all of it will fit into your budget.

If you want to advertise in trade publications, you'll need to know which ones will reach your intended audience; scout each publication to see layouts and how ads look in final printing or online. This is why it is also good to get yourself on your competitors' mailing lists to see what actually works and what doesn't.

Social media, such as Facebook, includes ads that can be tailored for certain markets, based on pay-per-click (ppc) and by the budget parameters you set for exactly when and for how long the ad will run, as well as other criteria. Advertising on Facebook and other such social media sites changes quickly, so you need to stay informed about the latest possibilities in this medium. There are many other considerations about advertising through social media that you most definitely did not learn in college, so you need to stay informed by reading the latest industry news in your area and staying abreast of what's currently hot. Asking your children or grandchildren what current "hot topics" you should be thinking about this week might help you get an idea of where to start.

You may decide that social media and trendy advertising techniques will not be the best way to sell your type of business, and that's fine too. Just don't cut yourself off from avenues that could help your business thrive because you refuse to investigate anything new.

Public Relations

Public relations (PR) definitely includes advertising, but it also involves long-term activities and image boosters for most businesses. If your business is event-oriented, you will be e-mailing, faxing, and sending press releases on a constant basis to news organizations, trade magazines, radio stations, and anyone who will listen to or read whatever you produce. If you're lucky, maybe they will even call you for an interview.

You may build some good PR by supporting or sponsoring your kids' or grandkids' sports teams or school activities. Almost all schools these days need outside help in order to field teams or produce plays or concerts, and most are willing to provide highly visible signs and banners or shout-outs in printed programs in exchange for your financial support.

If your business is events-oriented, you can use Facebook, Twitter, and other platforms to promote new events at the drop of a hat, although it must be carefully and tastefully done. No one wants promotions shoved in their faces, yet sending out a well-crafted blurb could easily translate into a turnout at an event like you've never seen before.

Public relations is all about getting the news out, however and wherever you can. With the Internet and social media, communicating has become so much easier and cheaper. You can find more details in a book I helped write, *Public Relations for Dummies,* which was published in 2006.

Now, let's take a brief look at some channels you should be considering when developing your marketing plan. If you plan carefully, you should be able to use most of these channels for both PR and advertising purposes.

World Wide Web

As has been discussed in previous chapters, in today's world you must have a website for your business. Through your website, you can provide basic information about who you are, what you do, and how you do it, or you can sell your goods directly—it all depends on what kind of business you are establishing.

But don't assume that just because you built a website, people will come to it. The World Wide Web isn't the Field of Dreams, you know.

There are two ways to drive traffic, or send people, to your website. One is organic (or free), whereby you get the traffic without any out-of-pocket expense. The other way is through paid methods, which will be discussed in more detail below.

The first thing you should do when building your website is conduct some keyword research on the words and phrases people might tend to use when searching for your product or service. Free or low-cost online tools are available for keyword research, including Wordtracker (www.WordTracker.com) and Google's keyword tool.

Once you know which words are most effective for your business, make sure those keywords are included in the copy on your website, especially in the text close to the top of each web page. Strategically weaving keywords into web copy is key in search engine optimization (SEO). You may want to hire a web copywriter to help you with this important step. The better your SEO, the more free traffic will come to your site.

Frequently posting fresh content on your site helps your ranking, too. This includes articles, blogs, and additional web pages. You can submit your articles to article banks and post comments with links to your blog on similar blogs in the hope of getting on their blogrolls and drawing some of those blogs' followers to your site.

Affiliate marketing is another way merchants can drive traffic to their sites. This arrangement is essentially a partnership with another online merchant or service provider, where you agree to let that affiliate sell your product on its website.

The affiliate earns a commission on the sale, and you make a sale you would not otherwise have gotten. Plus, you get the chance to market future products directly to this new customer. Affiliate marketing works best when the partnership is between complementary businesses whose target audiences share similar interests.

Many of the marketing methods discussed in this chapter are aimed at bringing visitors to your company's website. When they get there, your home page or landing page must instantly draw in these new prospects and make it easy for them to navigate their way around the site. Be sure to include on each web page an offer or other enticement to obtain the visitor's e-mail address. Give away a free report that has real value. It is the single biggest goal. If they click away without leaving their e-mail address, they most likely will not be back.

Depending on the nature of your business, a properly organized website, where orders can be placed around the clock using merchant accounts and auto-responder systems that process orders and send out confirmations (and even thank-you e-mails), can enable you to work fewer hours or work from remote locations (like on your laptop from a tropical island!).

Online Advertising

You can advertise your business directly on the Internet to increase the traffic, or visits, to your website. When done effectively, online advertising can transform your business from a one-stop shop for local customers to a worldwide store that's open 24/7 for anyone with a computer.

If you frequently update your website with fresh content that uses relevant SEO keywords, you will attract free, organic traffic to your site. But this process takes time and effort before your site rises to the top of the Google search page and gets noticed.

Paid Internet advertising methods can generate traffic and move your site to that first search page faster. Google AdWords is a popular pay-per-click Internet advertising system whereby Google places keyword-based ads for your business alongside the top results of Google keyword searches or on other related websites. Basically, you can get your business on the coveted first Google search page through a paid ad until your business can rise to that spot through the free, organic route.

The way it works is that you pay an agreed-upon price (flat rate per click or a bid-based rate per click) each time someone clicks on your ad. Note that you pay per click (PPC), not per sale.

So your website's landing page—where the Internet user is directed when they click on your ad—better be optimized and ready to close the sale. If it doesn't grab the new visitor's attention immediately and isn't easy to navigate, the viewer will click away quickly and be gone forever. Along with your pay-per-click ad budget.

You can control your PPC costs by setting budgetary and geographical limits in advance. One of the great benefits of AdWords is that it attracts prospects who have been specifically targeted—and are often ready to buy—to your site. You just have to have a site that is so well designed that it closes the deal.

Another Internet advertising system is Google AdSense. Here, you sign up for a free account, and Google places other company-relevant ads on your website at no cost to you. If a visitor to your site clicks through to one of these ads, the merchant pays Google per click and Google pays a portion of that fee to you.

E-mail Marketing

One of the easiest, most cost-efficient ways to market your new business is through e-mail marketing. Unlike direct mail, e-mail marketing has no printing, postage, shipping, or handling costs. And you have nothing to drag to the post office.

For as little as $15 per month or less, you can send bulk e-mail messages, often called "e-mail blasts," to your existing customers—as well as to potential customers—provided you have their e-mail addresses. One very popular e-mail marketing service, which also offers a free trial, is Constant Contact.

If your existing e-mail customer list is small and your budget allows for it, consider purchasing an e-mail list of people likely to be interested in your business services or products from a reputable list broker.

E-mail Blasts

E-mail blasts are a great way to interact with and retain your customers. By periodically "touching base" in a meaningful way that's beneficial to them, you can encourage their continued loyalty.

When you include interesting and relevant stories in your e-mails, your prospects can get to know you and your business better. Well-written stories are entertaining and informative. Stories are a great way to keep a reader's interest and ensure that future e-mails will be met with enthusiasm, opened, and read.

Teasers are another way to get a good ROI on your e-mail marketing campaign. For this to work, you need to know your target audience very

Word to the Wise

Don't underestimate the importance of good content in e-mail marketing. Provide your readers with some valuable offer, insights, information, or tips. When your e-mail list receives valuable, free information from you—without a hard sell attached—they will not only come to trust you, but they may also subconsciously feel like they "owe" you. If they benefit from your free tips, they will be more receptive to paying for some of your products and/or services.

well. You need to know what problems they need solved and what they care about most. Then you tease them by dangling the solution to their problem, or something else they really desire, in front of them—promising the solution if they click through on this link, which of course directs them to your landing page, where the sale can be closed.

Just be sure to balance your sales pitches with valuable freebies. You want your customers to open your e-mails and forward them to their friends (which will further expand your customer base). You don't want them unsubscribing or opting out because they see your e-mails as annoying, self-serving spam. If you notice a high rate of unsubscribers, cut back on the frequency of contact. If the rate doesn't improve, re-evaluate whether you're providing valuable content.

Because e-mail blasts are relatively brief, you may be able to handle the job yourself if you can't afford a professional copywriter. Use a conversational tone, as if you were talking to a friend, to increase your credibility and likability. No one likes to read stiff, formal copy—especially in their e-mail inbox.

The subject line is to e-mail blasts what the envelope is to direct mail. If the subject line doesn't pique your recipient's interest instantly, the e-mail may not even get opened. So, a perfectly worded e-mail blast may not even be read if the subject line is a dud. Subject lines should pique recipients' curiosity, promise a benefit they can't resist, or ask a question to compel them to open your e-mail.

In addition, e-mails are brief by nature. People don't have the same attention span when they are surfing the Web as they have when reading a handwritten letter or book. And, it seems everyone is short on time these days, with a ton of e-mails to sift through, and recipients are ever-ready to punch the delete button. Your e-mail blast must grab the reader's attention and make its point or pitch quickly before the reader moves on. Don't be too wordy. Instead, add links which bring the recipient to your website (or another location) where they can get additional information or free downloads.

E-mail blasts are also an effective way to survey your customers' needs and get feedback on what value they place on your e-mail stream. At the end of your e-mail, encourage the recipient to forward it to a friend. Ask them what they thought about it or what they'd like to see in future e-mails. Then, listen to the ones who respond and deliver.

E-newsletters

Newsletters can be another effective marketing tool for small businesses. They can be printed and distributed to a postal address, but these are more expensive because of the printing and mailing costs. Today, one of the most popular marketing methods is the e-newsletter. Like its cousin the e-mail blast, the e-newsletter is cheap and quickly produced. Inexpensive software services make it easy to create and e-mail professional-looking newsletters (as well as event invitations, cards, coupons and promotions) to your e-mail list—sometimes several times per month. Some popular e-mail marketing services include Constant Contact and Get Response.

These programs include hundreds of templates and thousands of images you can use to create professional-looking newsletters; fast delivery so your message remains timely and relevant; social media sharing so your message can reach beyond your current e-mail list; online surveys so you can stay on top of your customers needs; and tracking, analytics, and split testing so you know how effective your marketing really is and can determine an accurate ROI. Some even offer video-embedding capability.

Not long ago, all you had to do was offer a free newsletter and people would happily give you their e-mail address. But these days, free e-newsletters are a dime a dozen, and time is short. So, your e-newsletter should offer real value to the recipient if you expect them to opt in to receiving it. Sometimes, you need to almost give away the store just to get someone to subscribe so you can capture their e-mail address! Some businesses will give away e-books or other downloadable products of value, just to capture a person's e-mail address. In fact, most of the rules outlined regarding e-mail blasts also apply to e-newsletters.

How Bob Does It

I produced one print issue of my newsletter just as e-zines were becoming really popular, and then I got smart and switched to an e-newsletter.

Today, my e-newsletter goes out regularly to 65,000 subscribers. The subscriber list is managed and the newsletter distributed using Constant Contact.

I write the newsletter in Microsoft Word, and then my assistant formats it as text in an HTML shell for Constant Contact.

The content is a combination of original articles written by me plus short news or tips I take from other sources—fully attributed, of course.

Social Media

Rapidly becoming a force in the marketing of most any kind of business are social media platforms like Facebook, Twitter, LinkedIn, Google+, and Pinterest, just to name a few. It is now en vogue to let the world know what you are doing, eating, and buying several times per day. You may not understand or see the point in many of these new social media sites, but before you write them off completely, ask your kids or grandkids about them. They probably know about most of them and may give you some ideas about whether they think a particular social media avenue would be right for your business.

Facebook

Facebook (FB) is the largest and best-known social media platform. Although major companies are turning to FB ads and FB landing pages, Facebook is still primarily about socializing with friends and family. If you don't already have one, you should set up your own personal Facebook profile just to learn how everything works. Plus, it's a great way to keep up with your kids and brag about your grandkids.

Once you've figured out how Facebook works, create a business page, which you can link to your profile account but which operates as your business site. Your account settings will allow you to operate as yourself or as your business.

You can create a custom welcome page for your business account using an external tool called Pagemodo. Go to www.PageModo.com, create an account, and then you can choose to create a free page or subscribe to a small package allowing you more than one page and no advertising. It's a pretty nice application, and Pagemodo will give you a good start for your business look on Facebook.

You can also Google "Facebook applications" to see what else is out there, because social media changes daily.

Twitter, LinkedIn, and More

Another way to promote your business is through Twitter. If your followers tweet that they are going to your business that evening, it's not only free advertising, but it could entice their friends to join in the fun. These social media platforms provide ways to not only advertise your business, but to also better understand the needs of your target audience.

LinkedIn can help you network among professionals and potentially result in affiliate marketing opportunities. Groupon is a coupon-based social media platform designed to bring an influx of new customers to your business, at an initially discounted new customer rate. This is particularly effective in a slow economy, where bargain hungry shoppers are stretching their dollars.

Foursquare is a geographically based social media platform where participants can log in from their mobile devices at a participating business location, such as a restaurant or bar, and take advantage of posted specials or promotions by showing the business owner the special promotion on their mobile device. Maybe the promotion is half-price drinks or a free platter of wings. There are also big specials reserved for the "mayor"—the one person who has the most log-ins at your business. It's a way to reward your most loyal customer and encourage others to come in more often to try to become the mayor themselves! A win-win for the business owner.

Pinterest is a bulletin board-style social photo sharing website that allows users to create and manage image collections based around events, interests, hobbies, and any other type of item they enjoy or want to recommend. Users can browse other pinboards for inspiration, "re-pin" images to their own collections, or "like" photos. Some businesses, particularly those that sell fashion or craft items, use Pinterest to drive customers to their websites or create buzz about their products.

As you may know all too well, social media changes rapidly, and it can be hard to keep up with the changing tactics required to effectively take advantage of the various sites and trends—especially when you're busy running your business. To make the most of what social media can do for you, consider hiring a social media consultant to keep you ahead in the game of this necessary and rapidly-changing marketing goldmine.

Direct Mail

Don't think that the e-mail and social media are the only ways to market your business these days. One of the oldest and most successful ways to market your business is through direct mail—and it can still be a highly effective tool if used wisely. As its name implies, this method of marketing involves sending a written marketing piece or announcement directly to a prospect through the good, old-fashioned U.S. Postal Service.

If you're reading this book, you probably remember when we sent and received most of our communication through the mail. Now, the U.S. Postal Service is struggling because people use the mail so little. But just because we live in an age of advanced computer technology and social media, don't make the mistake of thinking there is no place in your marketing budget for the granddaddy of all marketing: the direct mail package.

In fact, according to the Direct Marketing Association website, "each dollar spent on direct marketing yields an average ROI of $11.73 versus $5.23 for non-direct marketing."

For a direct mail campaign to work, you first need to identify your target market—the people most likely to buy your goods or services. Then, get inside their minds. What motivates them? What are their problems and needs and how can your products or services help them? What emotional buttons can you push that will get them to trust, connect with, and respond to you?

Next, you need to buy or rent a mailing list of prospective targets to which you can forward your direct mail package. Not just any list, but a list of people identified as the most likely to be interested in your business. Contact a reputable mailing list service or list broker to make sure you get a quality list. The success of your marketing campaign depends on the quality of your list.

Equally as important as your mailing list is the quality of your copy and, to a slightly lesser degree, the graphics and design of your direct mail product. Direct mail marketing can take many different forms, from a simple postcard to a large multipage catalog or magalog.

There is a whole science surrounding the psychology of an effective direct mail package that involves the size, colors, and placement of text, photos, and captions, as well as the envelopes, fonts and layout used. These dynamics should be well understood by an experienced graphic designer.

But even the prettiest package won't be opened without the right words. Something must convert the recipient into a captive reader in the time it takes to walk from the mailbox to the trash can. Effective writing does that.

A professional copywriter can create a direct mail package that entices the recipient to open the envelope, keeps the reader hooked throughout the piece, and ultimately contains a "call to action" that the captive reader can't refuse. Omitting a call to action can sink your campaign. Don't assume your recipients know what do after they read your direct mail package. You have to tell them.

In your call to action, you specifically tell your recipient what to do: call a toll-free number, visit your website, subscribe to your newsletter, return a mail order, order online .... Be prepared to handle a potentially large response to your specific call to action, with adequate staffing or automated systems in place by the time the mailing goes out. Don't let poor follow-up or weak customer service undo the effectiveness of your campaign, or you may lose these new prospects as fast as you found them.

Advantages of direct mail marketing include being able to communicate with current customers, as well as targeting and converting potential new prospects. In addition, it offers the business owner great control over the copy, timing, and size of the campaign; the ability to split-test different marketing pieces; and the ability to measure the cost effectiveness of the whole campaign.

People are often more receptive to reading longer compelling pieces from their mailboxes than their inboxes. So, direct mail can be particularly effective when the recipient needs time to digest the material, such as in financial, medical, or technical copy, or where glossy photos or illustrations bring the sale home, as in landscaping, decorating, or even cosmetic surgery services. And, who doesn't like receiving a valuable coupon for a free or discounted service in the mail? Recipients can share a direct mail piece with others, leave it on the coffee table, or take it to the office.

There are some drawbacks to direct mail marketing. For example, the costs are higher than most web-based or social media marketing avenues. Changes to the copy can't be made cheaply either, especially if dealing with a larger-sized package. Printing, shipping, and handling charges can be expensive. Professionally trained copywriters and graphic designers can be found through organizations like American Writers & Artists Inc. or elance.com. If you want to self-publish, consider purchasing a desktop marketing software program.

So, how do you tell if a direct mail campaign is profitable? You must measure your return on investment, or "ROI." Simply put, this is the amount of money you've earned for each dollar spent on the campaign. In order to do this, you plug actual or estimated information relevant to the campaign into an ROI calculator. For an example of a free direct mail marketing ROI calculator program, see www.MarketingToday.com.

Your most effective direct mail marketing package will be referred to as your control; it's the one you will continue mailing out to new addresses to bring in new business. When another direct mail package mailing beats those results and brings you a higher ROI than your current control, then that mailing becomes your new control. Remember, there's a name for failed direct mail ... it's called junk mail.

Print Advertising

Print publications have been buffeted by the winds of change in recent years, which means print advertising is also in flux. But it can still be an effective form of getting your business noticed—depending on what kind of business you are running and where you choose to place your ads.

Two of the most common forms of print advertising are newspaper and magazine ads. Ads in trade publications are another. Like any other form of advertising, the primary purpose of the print ad is to sell your product or service. Projecting an image for your company (also known as "branding") and keeping your company's name and services in customers' minds are other reasons to consider print advertising.

In general, print advertising is expensive, and the ad space is confined. The biggest challenge is often in making the most of the very small window you have to grab the attention of the audience. Sometimes, you need to convey your message using only a photo and caption, so you must be sure the photo is effective enough to move the reader to the caption, and then be sure the caption is effective in conveying your message. Failure to do so means you just wasted your money.

Print ads are not about being smart in a gimmicky way but about being smart in a connecting-with-your-target-audience way. So, the first thing to do is make sure you get your message before the right audience.

For example, a magazine ad targeting young women would do better in *Good Housekeeping* than in *Field & Stream*, but may do its best in *Cosmo*. And a strictly local business, like a pizza shop, would spend its print ad budget more wisely by targeting local newspapers rather than regional ones. Ads in trade publications are another way to zero in on your target audience.

Benefits of print advertising include the ability to promote your company's unique selling proposition (USP) in a definitive, permanent, and portable way. Your USP is what makes your company better and different than your competition. A print message is less likely to be misread or misconstrued than e-mails or radio spots; it can be saved, filed, and referred to again and again, and it provides a vehicle for coupon offerings that can be carried around, shared, and otherwise distributed.

There are many industry tricks and psychological studies involved in creating effective print advertising and, because it is relatively expensive, it may pay to hire an agency to help. Your ROI can be affected by the photos you use, the captions, the copy, the offer, the call to action, your use of white space, colors, quotes, and other factors. Ads should contain a reference code to enable you to track their effectiveness.

Here are some of the questions you should ask yourself before you write your ad:

1. What are all the product benefits?
2. What are all the features of the product?
3. How is the product different and, hopefully, better than that of the competition?
4. What does the buyer expect when he or she plunks down a few dollars for the product? And do we deliver?
5. What methods, approaches, and sales techniques are the competition using?

6. How is the audience for my product different from the general public?
7. How much should my buyer reasonably expect to pay?
8. Does my average buyer have a credit card or a checking account?
9. Will my product be purchased for business or personal use?
10. Can I expect to get multiple sales from my buyers?
11. What is the logical "back end" product to sell someone, after he has purchased my product? ("Back end" refers to other products in your product line you can offer to someone who has bought the primary product featured in your ad.)
12. Will I need to show my product in color?
13. What's the "universe," or the total number, of potential customers?
14. Who will buy my product: teenagers or octogenarians, men or women, executives or blue-collar workers?
15. Is there a market for overseas sales?
16. Should I offer time payments?
17. Will my product be a good gift item?
18. Should my copy be long or short?
19. What should the tone of my copy be?
20. Should I test the price?
21. Should I test copy approaches?
22. Is there a seasonal market for my product and, if so, am I taking advantage of it?
23. Are testimonials available from satisfied customers?
24. Do I need photographs or illustrations?
25. Which appeals have worked in the past for this product?
26. What objections might arise from a prospective customer? How can I overcome these objections?
27. Should I use a premium?
28. Should I offer a money-back guarantee?

29. Is this item also sold by retail? Are there price advantages I can stress for buying direct from the ad?
30. Should I consider a celebrity testimonial?
31. Can I tie my copy to some news event?
32. Can I tie my copy to some holiday or seasonal event?
33. Does my product sell better in a particular region or climate?
34. Should I consider using a sweepstakes?
35. Can my product be sold through a two-step advertising campaign? (In a two-step campaign, ads generate inquiries rather than direct sales.)
36. What must I do to give the reader a sense of urgency so he or she will buy my product now?
37. Can I use scientific evidence in my sales approach?
38. Have I allowed enough time to write, design, and produce my ad and place my insertion order?
39. Can I get my customer to order by telephone?
40. What unsuccessful approaches have been used to try to sell this product?
41. Can I get powerful "before" and "after" pictures?
42. Assuming the ad is successful, am I prepared to fill all the orders?

Sales Brochures

We've all come across sales brochures at one time or other. Simply put, they are written materials that try to pique your interest in and/or sell you something.

There are many different formats of sale brochures, from simple fliers to large, glossy booklets, and the tone and copy combination can be either passive or active.

Maybe you saw a sales brochure at the library, or perhaps your doctor's office had some standing in a cardboard display begging you to "Take One." Such sales brochures that are just lying around, waiting patiently to be taken by anyone passing by, are passive marketing tools. They usually contain information that has a long "shelf-life," such as your basic firm

Word to the Wise

Sometimes testimonials from customers are included in these brochures to act like personal references for your business. If you save written thank-you notes from customers, you can pull complimentary text from them and—provided you get the customer's written consent—use it as a testimonial in your brochure or on your website.

background information, your product line, or an announcement about a new product or service.

Because writing, design, and printing costs can be expensive, businesses using these passive brochures should avoid including dated, time-sensitive, or fluctuating details (such as pricing information) so the brochure remains relevant for a long time.

However, sales brochures can also be an active marketing tool for your business if they target the correct audience and are written and designed in a manner that entices the recipient to open and read the brochure and then act on the call to action therein.

An effective sales brochure needs a catchy headline that immediately grabs the reader's attention. This is best done by promising to solve a reader's problem. To keep readers invested in reading your copy, they need to feel there's something in it for them. Ideally, you need to show them how they will benefit from using your business. Specifically, show how your goods or services will save them time, save them money, or make them money.

The brochure's copy must be compelling enough to maintain their interest. As they read along, your readers must believe that you will be able to deliver on your promise. Copy and photos with captions should complement each other, and the finished product should be laid out to effectively deliver your brochure's message to both kinds of readers: those who scan and those who read in detail.

Sales brochures can be farmed out to professional copywriters and/or graphic designers or may be created entirely in-house using a desktop publishing software program, such as the popular Print Artist Platinum, priced at about $50.

The 8½ x 11 trifold design is a popular and economical brochure for new small businesses because it is one page and it fits into a standard, business-sized mailing envelope. It's effective as a direct mailing as well as for presentations, trade shows, and leave-behind pieces.

A common mistake nonprofessional writers make is to load their brochures with a list of features, when they should instead be focusing on the benefits. In addition, they often overuse graphs, photos, and charts and make poor font, color, and other layout decisions that could negatively impact the business brand. Consider getting a graphic designer's guidance. Remember, you want your brochure to help—not hurt—your business.

Cold-Calling

Just the thought sends shivers down the spine. Is there anyone more hated than the annoying pest who interrupts your favorite show when you finally relax at the end of a long day? Now that you're in your own business, must you become an irritating nuisance, too? Must you make unsolicited, unwelcome calls to unsuspecting prospects?

Believe it or not, there is a place in a business marketing plan for cold-calling. Done right, cold-calling can generate new leads for your business. (Emphasis on "done right.") After all, if this didn't work at least part of the time, the calls would have stopped by now. So, how do you do this right?

The key to success is to cold call a *targeted* list, not to just open the phone book and start calling all the names beginning with "A." A targeted list includes prospects who are strangers to your business but who may reasonably be expected to be interested in your goods or services. You can obtain a targeted list from a vendor or pay a service to create a list of hot prospects for you based on research. Obviously, a customized list will cost more to procure.

Cold calling can be done by you or one of your employees, or it can be outsourced to an outbound telemarketing service provider. Most people do not feel comfortable making these intrusive calls and do not have a thick enough skin to take the nearly universal rejection and abuse in stride. Therefore, many business owners choose to outsource this job.

An outbound telemarketing service provider will train its staff in the details of your business and then create a campaign to generate new leads for your business. They will take the "cold" out of cold-calling by making the initial contact with new prospects, educating them on your services and qualifications, confirming their interest, and then forwarding you those leads who are "warm" and receptive to receiving a sales pitch from you.

Telemarketing

When most people hear the term "telemarketing," they think of those annoying, unsolicited phone calls from aggressive salesmen that interrupt dinner. But cold-calling, or outbound telemarketing, as previously discussed, is only one aspect of telemarketing.

Telemarketing can also be inbound in nature. Instead of generating new leads by making outbound cold calls, inbound telemarketing services your returning, existing, and new customers. If your direct mail, e-mail, website, and other marketing efforts result in an influx of new business, you will have to either hire the staff to service the demands or outsource the jobs to an inbound telemarketing service. Inbound telemarketing services include a virtual receptionist or answering service (instead of voice mail), appointment scheduling, customer service calls, and even fielding sales calls.

The benefits are many. It frees the business owner up to do other important nonadministrative work and allows the delegation of undesirable but necessary tasks. It provides the appearance of a larger staff to actual or potential customers without the payroll and other expenses associated with hiring additional office workers.

Telemarketing services can be customized for the individual needs of your business. Outsource as many or as few of these jobs as you'd like. Service providers will train their staff in the details of your business so they can competently represent your business on the phone. A good telemarketing service provider will leave your callers with the impression that they're speaking to one of your company's employees, not a service.

Sometimes the difference between making and losing a sale hinges on whether a human answers your phone. If a real person isn't available to help the caller when it's convenient for the caller, she may find a competitor who can. For the busy, new small-business owner, telemarketing services may be the next best thing to cloning yourself.

Referral Marketing System

Word-of-mouth referrals are great. But they alone are not enough to grow your business. You still need a system in place to manage referrals and strategies to convert them from leads to clients. And then, you need strategies to repeat the process so your referral source base continues to grow and generate more referrals.

You can purchase a referral marketing system online, but if you would rather skip that expense right now, you need to set up your own system. First, you should identify your ideal client or customer and then think of people or businesses that may be in a position to refer people to your business. This is the basis of many business networking groups.

Next, you have to find a way to actually ask for the referral, a sometimes uncomfortable hurdle to overcome. Ask your referral sources what you could do to make it easy for them to refer your business to others. Do they want your business cards? Your website or e-mail address? Maybe your business has, or needs, a free app for mobile phones and such devices?

Give the referral source an incentive to refer business to you. This can be anything from a monetary reward or referral fee (if ethical), a discount, a reciprocal new business referral, recognition, and/or a simple thank you. In fact, the most important thing you can do to thank a referral source is to do a good job and not abuse the trust they put in you when they recommended the client to you.

Be sure to set up a system using your calendar or contact management programs to keep track of these leads, especially those who don't convert to customers immediately. You should have a system to follow up on the lead in the future and a system to update the referral source when the lead eventually converts to a client.

Straight Talk from Bob

You know that for your marketing to work, it must tap into a powerful emotion the buyer is experiencing. The emotions most commonly targeted in copy are greed, guilt, fear, and exclusivity. Of course, there are many others: love, hate, envy, joy, empathy, and benevolence, for instance.

I've identified four other emotions that work for a wide variety of offers, but especially for business opportunity and money-making offers. They are desire, dissatisfaction, disappointment, and despair. I call them the "4 Ds." There are many similarities between the Ds, but subtle differences, too:

Desire. Prospects who respond to business opportunity and money-making offers want something. Not just a little. They crave its possession. For some prospects, the desire is for money or material objects—a boat, vacation home, luxury car—and they need money to own it. For many, it's the difference that money can make in their lives:

the ability to run your own business, quit your 9-to-5 job, or get rid of money worries for good. Others desire the security and peace of mind they think financial independence will bring. Promising the fulfillment of the prospect's prominent desire is a powerful way to entice him to pull the trigger and invest in your product.

Dissatisfaction. Countless individuals slog through life, unhappy and dissatisfied with their lot. They want something better, but are often unclear on what that would be or how to achieve it. In business opportunity marketing, our selling proposition is that we will help you make the money you need to live the life you want to live. In self-help and spiritual marketing, the promise is often to show you how to be happy and fulfilled by who you are and what you have.

Dissatisfaction is a potent emotion to tap into. Dissatisfaction is emotional pain. People act mainly for two reasons: to attain pleasure and avoid pain. Of these, the avoidance of pain can be stronger than the attainment of pleasure. Another way to put it is that people act for only two reasons: to gain reward and avoid punishment.

Disappointment. What's the difference between dissatisfaction and disappointment? Dissatisfaction means the prospect has a problem he has not solved or a situation he cannot resolve—for example, he wants to own a BMW, but can't afford it. Disappointment is more specific. It means the prospect has tried to solve the problem or resolve the situation—and it hasn't worked out. The disappointed prospect is wary of marketing claims. That makes him highly skeptical and difficult to sell to. It's far easier to market to prospects who have had some degree of success solving their problem and want more help.

Despair. Despair means the prospect's situation is so dire, it is emotionally painful. The prospect feels no one can help him and there is no hope. The best approach here is to prove that what you offer does in, fact work, and has worked for many of your customers. Testimonials, case studies, and YouTube videos are three obvious marketing tactics for proving your claims. There are others; e.g., show images of checks you have received as a result of using your money-making system.

You may think the 4 Ds—desire, dissatisfaction, disappointment, and despair—are too negative. But negative marketing can work. Fear is a powerful motivator. It's not universally right for every marketing campaign. But next time you're formulating your promotional strategy, see if you can build a message around one of the 4 Ds.

13

Becoming a Thought Leader in Your Niche

All else being equal, prospects hire the vendor or buy from the businessperson they perceive as an expert in his or her niche or specialty. If you are a 50+, setting up a business in a field in which you have been working for years, you have a big head start in this area. You probably ARE an expert in your specialty, and you've got a body of work—and the gray hairs—to prove it.

Now, you just need to prove your expertise to your new potential clients, who may not know about your past exploits. This chapter will provide you insight on what you can do to become a widely recognized guru in your field—and why you should want to become one.

Build Your Platform

Building a reputation or, as some call it, a "platform" as a guru is not a pat-yourself-on-the-back party. It is not a popularity contest. And it isn't about what a great writer you are. The world is full of great writers whose works never see the light of day. And, although it isn't about who you know, knowing people certainly helps.

It works like this: As your expertise becomes more widely known, your visibility will increase. As your visibility increases, your credibility will increase until you become valuable to more and more clients.

A platform, then, describes all the ways you are visible and appealing to a future, potential, or actual audience. It is your promise that you will perform. Your platform includes, but is not limited to, the web presence you maintain, public speaking you do, classes you teach, articles you write, information products you develop, and organizational boards you serve on.

One example of a strong platform is that of Anthony Robbins—famous for fire walking and motivational seminars—with his infomercials and public seminars. Not only does he produce infomercials, he also writes books and has a strong web presence. On his website, he sells his products, including supplements, a rapid planner kit, information CDs, DVDs, meditation music CDs, and financial success mixed media. He also advertises upcoming events you can sign up for. And he has a newsletter you can subscribe to and a "community" you can join. That is a strong platform.

And, of course, you've heard of or seen Dr. Phil on TV. He, too, has a strong web presence where his fans can view past episodes of his show, see a summary of upcoming shows, contact him, apply to be on a future show, and purchase his products. You'll find books by not only Dr. Phil, but by other respected authors. Because of his visibility, he was able to get a book published that quickly achieved best-seller status.

These men, and many other men and women, have built platforms and become recognized experts in their fields. You can, too.

Benefits of Being a Guru in Your Field

Volumes have been written about selling and marketing, especially for entrepreneurs, small businesses, and self-employed professionals. But there is one marketing strategy that, if you master it, eliminates the need to do any other type of selling or marketing ever: building a platform by becoming a recognized expert in your niche.

This is one place where being over 50 should be an advantage for you: Not only do you know more people and have more experience in your field, but your age alone can make you seem more "expert." Most people find it a bit hard to believe that a 20-something entrepreneur has all the secrets, and they would rather listen to someone who has been around long enough to see difficulties and figure out how to overcome them.

How does proving yourself as an expert in your field virtually ensure you a long-term sustainable marketing advantage over your competitors?

We live in the Information Age, an era in which we are bombarded by data and drowning in information, yet starved for knowledge. Although information is more plentiful and available than at any other time in history (thanks largely to the Internet), people are overwhelmed by information overload and unable to process it all. Increasingly, we look to experts who seem to have a handle on this information (or at least on a segment of it in a particular field) and who can help us make sense of the data and guide us in our actions.

If you position yourself as the information expert in a particular topic or subject, people needing help with this topic or subject turn to you first. Here's how you benefit when you become an expert in your field: You create an immediate, overwhelming demand for the products or services you sell. If one-third of a market of a million people is favorably predisposed to buy from experts, the expert in that market has 333,333 prospects vying for attention.

Since the demand for your services as a recognized expert in your field far outstrips the supply (most people can handle far fewer than 333,333 consulting assignments and speaking engagements), there's no need to get out and hustle for new business: You have prospects coming to you instead of you having to go to them. This eliminates the need to do most types of conventional marketing, such as advertising or cold-calling.

Since you do not have to spend time marketing or selling yourself, you can spend more of your time on billable work. So your income increases. Another benefit of demand outweighing supply is that you no longer have to negotiate your fees. With so many people vying for the few slots available on your schedule, you have the luxury of taking only those who can pay your full fee and turning away all other inquiries. Your prices go up, and your revenue increases even more.

Having the demand for your services far outstrip the supply gives you the luxury of being selective. You can select only the assignments that interest you, and work only with the clients you like. Not only will you

Word to the Wise

The greater your status, the less likely clients are to question your work, advice, or judgment. This can be a double-edged sword. On the one hand, it frees you to give straightforward advice, regardless of whether the client agrees or is pleased by it. And it eliminates the headache of clients who argue with or challenge you. On the other hand, you risk getting arrogant to the point where you close yourself off to what may be valuable client input. No one, including experts, can possibly know everything.

enjoy your work more, but your success rate will likely be higher because you are doing work you are good at for people you like (and who like you).

Picking Your Niche

Recognized experts are not born, they are "manufactured" through self-marketing and promotion. After years of building your experience and learning lessons the hard way, you may find that sentiment slightly offensive or you may recognize its truth—or both. But realize that marketing yourself as an expert does NOT mean you need to fabricate stories about your experience, ideas, or wisdom. It just means you need to know how to demonstrate to everyone else that you do have the expertise you claim to have. You need to understand the philosophy, attitude, and action plan you must implement to elevate yourself to expert status and to build a strong platform.

The key philosophy behind becoming an expert and, thus, building a platform is one of acceptance. Specifically, you should accept the fact that we live in an expert-oriented society and that there will be experts in virtually every field of knowledge, and when you have accepted that concept, you can decide that since there's going to be experts or gurus in your field, you might as well be one of them.

Whether you think the adulation many people lavish upon gurus and celebrities is justified or absurd is, frankly, irrelevant. That recognized experts and celebrities are looked up to is simply the reality of life, and this is a chapter about dealing with reality and being successful in the world as it is, not as you or others wish it would be.

Recognizing that the business world is expert-driven—and that expert status can be yours if you work at it—is the first step to becoming recognized as a leading expert in your field.

"See yourself as a brand and learn techniques to distinguish yourself from others," writes Roz Usheroff in *Speakers Gold*. "Developing brand distinction builds your reputation and opens the door to future promotions, opportunities, and options."

How to Establish Your Guru Reputation

Alan Kay, a Disney fellow at Walt Disney Imagineering Research and Development, sums up the methodology used to building your platform as a recognized expert: "You make progress by giving your ideas away; businesspeople haven't learned this yet."

To truly establish yourself as an expert and set yourself ahead of the pack, you have to conduct an ongoing program of self-promotion in which information dissemination is the primary vehicle. Chances are you already have substantial knowledge in one or more specialized areas, just by living and working for several decades. Now you need to figure out how to take that specialized knowledge and use it to build your own image, which can enhance your business.

"The great mistake of most small-business people is to imagine that their detailed knowledge of their niche market is widely dispersed," writes Gary North in *Remnant Review* (April 20, 2001, p. 5). "On the contrary, hardly anyone knows it. They are owners of a capital asset that others do not possess and have no easy way of possessing it."

The knowledge you have gained will serve as the base of your platform, but experience alone is not enough. You have to augment your knowledge base with further research and study.

How Bob Does It

I am not an academic, but I consider myself a scholar, or at least a student, of my topic: direct mail. I attend workshops and conferences, subscribe to industry periodicals, study the direct mail that crosses my desk each day, read numerous books on direct marketing, and regularly exchange results on what's working with clients, colleagues, and competitors.

Therefore, when I offer myself as a leading expert to clients, I do it with a clear conscience, knowing I have done everything in my power to make that claim legitimate. Am I the undisputed best direct mail copywriter in the world? No. But I constantly strive to be the best direct mail copywriter I can be, which is all anyone can ask.

Surprisingly, most people don't do that—they don't try to be the best. A. L. Williams, the life insurance magnate, once said, "You beat 90 percent of the people just by being good. Beating the other 10 percent is a dog fight." Even if you do not reach the level of "recognized expert" that you think you deserve, simply striving for excellence in a world where most do not will set you far ahead of 90 percent of the pack.

You should have solid knowledge of your topic, but you need not possess earth-shattering new data, breakthrough methodology, or unique secrets. To establish yourself as an expert, the main requisite is to present what you know—the latest thinking, proven principles or best practices—in a clear, interesting, accessible fashion. There's an old saying that "experts don't know more than anyone else; it's just that their information is better organized."

Choose—or Create—Your Niche

You want to be an expert and build a platform—but about what? You need to have a clear picture of both your subject and your market. A niche is a cross between a topic (quality, design for manufacturability, management) and an industry (automotive, plastics, paints and coatings).

Experts find their niches in one of two ways: on purpose or by accident. For instance, there are marketing consultants galore. But I once met a consultant who specialized in the niche of marketing for car washes. He had created his own niche on purpose.

He knew marketing and had a business background, but he had also owned and operated a couple of successful car washes. He had found a niche where he could be credible and successful and not have to compete with all the marketing generalists out there. With thought, you can probably find two to three or more niches where you can become an expert and build a credible platform.

Other people, like self-promotion expert Ilise Benun, fall into a niche largely by accident. Here's how Ilise tells it (from a personal conversation, which can be found in my book *The Six Figure Consultant*):

> *I was fired from the second (and last) real job I ever had. I had been working for a year and a half in the New York office of a family-owned, Kenyan safari company. I was hired thanks to my best friend, but ours had always been a rocky friendship and working together, I know now, wasn't a great idea.*
>
> *One Friday in April 1988, I was called into the conference room by the Big Boss—in reality, a small, silent type not given to emotional outbursts. He sat down at the table, handed me an envelope and said, "Thank you very much." At first I didn't understand what was happening. He couldn't possibly be firing me, but he was, and when I finally got it through my head, I was livid! "I will never work for anyone again," I vowed to anyone who'd listen.*

Indeed, I had no plan, so I got busy trying to figure out what to do. In terms of my skills and talents, my degree in Spanish seemed useless because I didn't want to work for the U.N. However, I was the most organized person I knew (still am), and all of my artsy friends were completely and utterly disorganized (though they aren't so much anymore). So, I came up with the fancy and (I thought) original title of Professional Organizer and got busy telling everyone what I did. (In other words, I started networking!) Before long, I had a few clients willing to pay $15 an hour to have me sit with them and pick through their mountains of clutter, one piece at a time.

It was strangely therapeutic, though very slow going, and, little by little, I began to notice a pattern: Buried under each person's pile, there was inevitably one piece of paper representing some little self-promotion task they were neglecting. Once we'd unearthed that phone message or note from someone asking for information, I'd say, "Let's write them a letter describing your work," or "Why don't we send them those slides?" I certainly didn't know marketing, but to me, it seemed like nothing more than common sense. It didn't take me long to realize that the clutter was not the problem, but merely the intentioned obstacle people used to protect themselves from the responsibility of self-promotion.

Over the course of the next few years, I evolved from Professional Organizer to Self-Promotion Specialist, learning from my own mistakes and those of my clients, practicing what I preached—and "preaching" by running my little self-promotion empire out here in Hoboken, New Jersey.

Ilise is now a successful speaker, author, and consultant in the field of self-promotion. She publishes an excellent newsletter on the topic, *Marketing Mentor*. You can learn more about her and the advice she has to offer at www.Marketing-Mentor.com.

So, the decision you must make is whether to establish yourself as an expert within an existing specialty or niche or to create your own.

The first option is to become recognized in a known industry or subject: quality control, object-oriented analysis, database marketing, sales, customer service, interpersonal skills, time management, or stress reduction.

The advantage of this first option is that, since everyone recognizes and understands the topic, they can easily understand what you do. And there is a built-in demand for experts—a huge, ready market of people who want help with quality, time management, or whatever.

The disadvantage is that since you are not the first person to be attracted to the field, you have competition. You share your expert status with other specialists, which will make it more difficult to develop your reputation and build a platform.

The second option is to invent a category or niche in which you will become the preeminent specialist. Usually, this invention is cosmetic or semantic rather than actual.

"By inventing words, your ideas will seem fresh whether they are or not," writes Emilie Rutherford in *CIO* magazine. People invent a new buzzword, theory, or jargon, then claim ownership of it. Examples include Michael Hammer's "re-engineering" and Tom Peters' "liberation management."

I once had a meeting with the business partner of an expert in the negotiating field. He told me, "Our success is due to the fact that we invented negotiating as a topic." I asked him to explain. He answered:

> *The [expert] began his career as a lawyer. One day he woke up and said, "What I really do is negotiate all day; it just happens to be in the area of law."*
>
> *He realized that negotiation, which lawyers have to become skilled at, is central to almost every facet of life. Based on this realization—that everything is negotiation and lawyers are negotiation specialists—he changed his focus from law practice to teaching corporate managers to use negotiation skills to get what they want in business.*

The advantage of inventing your own niche is that, if the concept, term, theory, or buzzword catches on, you "own" the category. You are by default the leading expert in the field. You "own" your niche. That gives you an extremely strong platform.

The disadvantage, or risk, is the likely possibility that the buzzword you invent does not catch on and that people do not understand what it means. If you promote yourself as the expert in "hyper-communication," and no one knows what the term means or even wants to learn what it means, you gain no advantage.

How Bob Does It

While I recognize the "invent-a-term" strategy is extremely powerful, I have avoided it for two reasons that may or may not hinder your own pursuit of it.

First, my mind doesn't work that way. I am good at packaging information and working within a known field, but I am not a pioneer or revolutionary thinker. In all my life, I have had neither a brilliant original concept nor a nifty jargon to go with it.

Second, the invent-a-term experts are happy to invent and use buzzwords, which oppose my plain-speaking nature.

When a buzzword or new jargon becomes part of the language and culture, the inventor benefits enormously. But until it does, he is speaking in doublespeak whenever he uses his jargon in lectures and writing. Even after the buzzword is accepted, it often does not communicate its concept as clearly as a plain English phrase would.

I prefer clear writing, clear thinking, and plain speaking. And I think a plain-speaking approach conveys a sense of credibility, trust, and integrity to your audience. "Never use jargon words like reconceptualize, demassification, attitudinally," writes David Ogilvy in *The Unpublished Ogilvy* (Crown Publishers, 1984). "They are the hallmarks of a pretentious ass."

There is one other problem with inventing your own terms: Because others do not know your term, no one is searching for it on Google. Therefore, there is little or no online demand for your new made-up specialty. This, in turn, hinders your efforts to build a list and otherwise build your platform online.

Your Guru Action Plan

Once you decide whether you want to set yourself up in a long-recognized niche or to try to promote a new one, the process for becoming recognized as an expert in that niche is the same. Follow these steps to get yourself moving down the guru path:

1. **Write articles.** Writing articles for print publication or the web is the quickest and easiest way—and usually the first step—in building your reputation.

2. **Produce and sell information products.** Experts are focal points of information on a specific topic, and they enhance their reputations as experts by producing and marketing "information products" on these topics. This includes audiotapes, videos, CD-ROMs, software, directories, resource guides, special reports, market research, booklets, pamphlets, and more.

3. **Publish a newsletter or e-zine.** A powerful technique for building your reputation with a defined audience over a period of time is to regularly send them a newsletter, which can either be free or by paid subscription.

4. **Make speeches.** Giving keynote speeches at meetings and conventions quickly establishes your reputation as an expert.

5. **Give seminars.** Virtually every recognized expert gives seminars, both to reach new prospects and to solidify his or her position as a leading expert. Speeches are short talks, typically an hour long. Seminars, in comparison, are more comprehensive presentations, ranging from a half-day to three days. Even better is the newest version of the seminar, the teleseminar: It takes only an hour to present, and neither you nor your audience has to leave home.

6. **Conduct a public relations campaign.** Attract the print and broadcast media—newspapers, magazines, radio, TV—to interview you and feature you in stories relating to your area of expertise.

7. **Use the Internet.** Another central component of establishing yourself as an expert is building a web presence, the centerpiece of which is a website that is both an information resource and a community of interest on a subject relating to your core expertise.

8. **Achieve critical mass.** Critical mass is the point where the business payoff from the tasks completed in your platform action plan are able to sustain long-term results, above and beyond each short-term promotion.

9. **Maintain expert status.** As an expert, you can't rest on your laurels. The world is changing constantly, and the leader in any field must change with it or be left far behind. You must work continually to maintain your status, or you may lose it.

Four Phases of Platform Building

There are four phases in the process of developing your platform as an expert: the start-up phase, growth phase, critical mass phase, and maintenance phase.

Start-up Phase

In your start-up phase, you begin implementing your action plan. At this stage, any interest generated in you and your services is specifically linked to each promotion. You write an article; you get a few phone calls. You give a speech; a few potential clients give you their business cards after the presentation and express interest in learning more about who you are and what you do.

If you stop promoting yourself—no new seminars, no new client newsletters, no new articles—people forget about you, and the inquiries stop flowing. You have not yet built up awareness of your reputation to the point where people think of you even if you are not running some type of promotion.

Growth Phase

In stage two, the growth phase, you still run a series of promotions as outlined in the platform building action plan, but now you see synergy between the various efforts. You give a speech and someone in the audience, in post-lecture conversation, compliments you on your white paper. Or, a prospect you have been referred to takes your call because he reads your e-newsletter and is impressed by what you write. The individual tasks in the action plan begin to feed one another. You get a synergy in which the total impression is greater than the sum of the individual communications.

Critical Mass Phase

Stage three is the critical mass phase. In nuclear physics, critical mass is the point where a nuclear reaction becomes self-sustaining; the reaction does not have to be fueled but continues to generate tremendous energy on its own.

In platform development, I define "critical mass" as the point where your name is out in the marketplace so much, so often, that people are continually aware of who you are and what you do. You are getting a steady flow of inquiries that would continue even if you stopped promoting yourself for a time. People have heard of you and know who you are. When they contact you, they are predisposed to buy your services and do not have to be "sold" on doing so. Your lead volume is high, and you get numerous leads that you cannot trace to a particular promotion; people just seem to hear about you and call you.

Maintenance Phase

Stage four is maintenance: doing a level of promotion required to keep yourself at critical mass. This level is not as high as required in phase one or two, but it's not zero, either. You can't totally rest on your laurels. Competition and a changing environment necessitate that you make a deliberate effort to maintain your leading-edge status.

Somewhere between stage three and stage four, you will possess a platform large and strong enough to convince a publisher to offer you a book contract. You will have all the evidence you need to support a strong platform. And you'll have taken all the necessary steps to help with marketing a book. This ability makes publishers happy and more willing to take a chance on you.

And, after you have one or more books published in your field, you will gain even more credibility as an expert—which beautifully feeds the cycle and allows you to continue to enhance your status.

The Rule of Seven

How often must you market yourself to achieve expert status? How much exposure do you need? A good rule of thumb is the "Rule of Seven." First stated by marketing consultant Jeffrey Lant, the Rule of Seven says you should reach your target market seven times within an 18-month period.

Although somewhat arbitrary, the Rule of Seven is a good starting point. The table on the next page indicates the minimum number of times you should perform action tasks based on where you are in the platform development process.

At the beginning, in the start-up phase, you typically spend a lot of your time marketing and launch a barrage of promotions in a relatively short period of time. Making a splash with a flurry of frequent self-promotion gets attention and makes your name stand out. Since you're just starting out, an added benefit of this phase is that all this activity produces materials you can reprint as sales literature for yourself or your firm.

Frequency of Action Plan Tasks Based on Phase in Development	
Phase	**Frequency of Self Promotion**
Start-up	4 to 6 times within 3 to 6 months
Development	Every other month
Critical mass	Quarterly
Maintenance	2 to 3 times per year

After a few months of heavy marketing activity, you'll begin to build a collection of promotional materials—reprints of bylined articles, seminar announcements, press clippings, reviews, audio CDs, and DVDs. Now, you can use those materials as you move through the other phases, in addition to the new materials you continue to create.

Straight Talk from Bob

Recently, I have been getting a spate of e-mails from Red Lobster inviting me to eat there. Based on the frequency, I suspect they are spam, though I may be wrong.

Either way, they are reaching the wrong audience with me, because—odd though it may be—I don't like lobster. I have no patience with cracking the shell to get the meat. I figure that any creature bothering to evolve armor to keep me out deserves to be left alone.

If you are trying to become an expert in your field, you can't afford, like Red Lobster, to spend much time or effort on products or services outside of your specialty. Reason: The response rate will be unprofitable and people will be offended or stop listening to you.

I know this because I tested it once. I created an e-book, all from public domain information, called *Cheap Car Tips and Tricks*, showing how to save money on everything from repairs to gas. You can view my landing page here: www.CheapCarTips.com. I then did an e-mail blast to my newsletter subscriber list.

We sold maybe three copies. In addition, we got e-mails in response that said things like: "Bob, I subscribe to your e-mails for marketing tips, not car information. What do you know about cars anyway?"

I have seen repeatedly that the better targeted a product is to the interests of my subscribers, the more sales I will make. Conversely, when I do an affiliate deal for a product I like (say a book on success written by a colleague) but that is not 100 percent focused on marketing or entrepreneurship, sales are mediocre at best.

You may be thinking: "Duh, Bob. This isn't exactly rocket science. It's painfully obvious, even to a dolt like you."

Maybe. But I see this rule violated every day. I also get requests from people all the time asking me to promote stuff to my list that my subscribers would have no possible interest in—ranging from vitamins to children's books.

If you want to establish your expertise, focus your content and products with laser-like intensity on your specialty topic. That is a key to establishing yourself and to making money in Internet marketing.

In the meantime: Anybody out there want to buy a book on cars?

14

Operating as a Virtual Company

As your business grows, you may need help running it. If you hire employees to work on-site, the business will quickly outgrow your home, forcing you to lease office space and deal with rent, commuting, and other hassles. Maybe you do want to get out of the house, but if you don't, the solution is to run your business as a virtual office where employees telecommute and vendors work from their own offices connected to yours via the Internet.

This chapter shows the advantages of running a virtual office, as I do, and it presents step-by-step instructions on hiring the help you need and setting them up to work virtually.

What is a virtual office? Simply put, a virtual office staff doesn't work in a physical location with you. They work online, for your company, doing tasks that regular office personnel would do. From their homes or other remote offices, they can provide a variety of services, such as:

- Handling your mailings
- Supplying administrative office support
- Answering phones in your name
- Organizing files
- Managing your office
- Providing a business address
- Offering receptionist services
- Writing collateral marketing materials

- Setting up and maintaining your website
- Planning travel
- Providing meeting support
- Assisting with communications
- Managing projects and other tasks

Before the Internet age, outsourcing office work was done by companies on an occasional basis because of work overloads or to save money. Outsourcing has long been recognized as a low-cost way to get work done without hiring full-time people. You can pass those savings on to customers or increase your profits. There are scads of temporary employment agencies to meet that need.

Now, the Internet is an expected office standard, and wise companies use it daily. Almost everything can be done online. Contracts can be signed with one keystroke. Payments can be made online, and e-mail confirmations are valid records. Conversations can take place through typing. Conferences can occur between several offices at once, saving time and travel expenses. It's not the wave of the future, it's the *now*.

It's also one less strain on a business start-up budget. You can concentrate on running your business, trusting the virtual vendors to do the rest. Most virtual offices are affordable, starting around $14.95 per month for a business address and mail support through a company such as Mailbox Forwarding.

Three Types of Virtual Office Help

Most virtual offices use some or all of these types of workers. For purposes of telling them apart, I use abbreviations. They are:

- Virtual assistants (VA)
- Virtual office personnel (VOP)
- Auxiliary virtual help (AVH)

You may want help in all three areas or just one. It depends on your budget and your needs. If you have a lot of capital to start your business and are not personally comfortable with technology, you may want to consider drawing from each group.

WORD TO THE WISE

There is no standardized definition for the terminologies used to describe virtual employees, as different companies use the same terms to describe different roles. So, make sure you know exactly how a company defines a particular term before you end up hiring a worker who won't do what you need.

VIRTUAL ASSISTANTS (VA)

Virtual assistants usually don't answer your phone or act as a receptionist. They are administrative experts, acting as the backbone for the office, providing office support. Your assistant will consult with you, learn your business—its needs and goals—and make a plan to help you meet them. Then he or she can tell you how to move forward, working with you to achieve that plan. The VA provides continuity and task support, organizes everything to run smoothly, and can help you set up security to make sure everything your virtual office does is private and protected.

For example, the VA doesn't write your marketing plan; you need a marketing expert for that. But a VA can take your marketing plan and help you follow through with it. VAs are experts in the technology needed to post blogs, set up e-newsletters, manage subscriptions, manage autoresponder systems, and setting up social networking applications and tools. They can plan your travel and provide meeting support.

Writing social postings and blogs is not a job for your VA, but a VA can set up the technology for you to be able to post. And VAs can help you find vendors to do the work that they don't do. In other words, a VA's job is to help you set up your office with all the things you need and want to use to do your business. A virtual assistant is there to help you get your business off the ground and to keep you on a charted course.

To find virtual assistants, check out businesses such as Davinci Virtual and Virtual Assistant Networking. Assistu.com also offers information on VAs, and the starting price for its services is about $30 an hour.

If you are unsure of all that is involved in starting a virtual office, hiring a virtual assistant is probably the place you want to start. And, after your business is settled and growing, virtual assistants help with finding affiliates for your website and managing joint partnerships.

Certification for a VA, according to VirtualAssistantCareerGuide.com, isn't as important as experience. However, if a VA wants training, there are many avenues to get it. Certification comes through two degrees: Certified Professional VA and Certified Master VA. The programs are intense, so if you are thinking of hiring anyone with those certifications, you know they will be well-qualified.

Virtual Office Personnel (VOP)

Virtual office personnel are secretarial assistants, providing the types of services that you need to run your office daily. They will answer the phone for you, take care of your mailings and faxes, set appointments, act as receptionists, and keep track of your data and files.

Some companies that specialize in providing virtual office personnel may also provide meeting and conference facilities. They allow total flexibility in the way you want to conduct your business. If you have a business that you can run while sunning on the beach, they can make you look and sound like you have a corner office in Manhattan—simply by giving you a business address, answering your phone with a live person, and providing a live place to meet with clients.

Davinci Virtual, Intelligent Office, and Office Scape can provide these services, as can others that specialize in certain services, such as www.CallRuby.com, which supplies receptionists. But they all do mostly the same thing. Their services center around answering the phones, taking orders, scheduling, etc.

Office Scape has many different office options. It also offers Virtual Office 2.0 web applications, which is a free office portal that allows you to manage all of your virtual web applications, including managing your users, user access, and online payments. It has four different offerings for a virtual office or a physical one, starting at about $58 a month for a nomadic office that can be operated anywhere. It even has a do-it-yourself office, where you custom design an office to meet your specific needs.

Regus.com offers everything needed to set up your virtual office except your VA in different package plans, starting at $169 a month. You can also reach Regus and others through hq.com, which provides a comprehensive array of services and 750 locations all over the world.

Auxiliary Virtual Help (AVH)

This category includes any other services you need to run your business. You may need someone to build and host a website. To decide what marketing you need to do, you may need to hire a marketing consultant. Almost every business needs someone to write collateral marketing materials, such as brochures, newsletters, postcards, press releases, and most businesses could use help with web and logo design and search engine optimization. Freelance writers can also help with social network postings and blogs—which are important parts of business, today.

These services aren't involved in the day-to-day running of the business, as receptionists and secretaries are, but you will likely need them at times. You can easily find this kind of help online, and it can all be handled online. If you have a VA, he or she can help you establish exactly what you need and find the resources for it. Elance.com and CraigsList.com are also places to find freelance workers for all AVH needs. Looking in the Yellow Pages under "secretarial services" should lead you to workers in your area; when you contact these local workers, tell them you want work to be done off-site.

How Bob Does It

When I hired my first administrative assistant, I didn't know how or where to find one. So I picked up a copy of our local weekly Pennysaver (newspaper) and saw a few ads under the SERVICES category for typing and word processing services. I called a few and said, "I'd like to talk to you about buying 30 hours of your time a week." They were all eager to get the job. The first one didn't work out, but the second did.

I found my copywriting project manager by attending a local marketing conference where she was one of the speakers. I was so impressed with her I said, "How would you like to represent me and handle all the selling of my copywriting services?" And she has done so ever since.

I found my Internet marketing manager when a woman who worked as an admin for my computer service company quit because she was moving to the other end of the state. When I heard, I called her and said, "How would you like to work with me on an hourly basis?" And she has ever since.

Pros and Cons of a Virtual Office

The Advantages

For some services, virtual office staff is on the job 24/7. You train them to understand your company's needs so they know how to help you. For instance, if you are in sales and marketing, they can screen your calls to your specifications, lining up only true prospects for you. VAs and VOPs can do their work, depending on what it is, from smartphones, personal digital assistants, and laptop computers. You can focus on their performance instead of whether they are on task all the time, as you would if they were in your office.

It eliminates the worry of whether employees will show up to work. Traditional job hiring and employee human resources headaches are nonexistent in a virtual world, as are healthcare costs, employee taxes, insurance issues, and unemployment compensation.

You may never even speak to your virtual staff. Communication can be handled online through e-mail.

You can operate from anywhere. Your virtual receptionist or call center will handle the calls. You can work from anywhere, and your callers will never hear your kids screaming in the background or seagulls squawking if you're on the beach. This is also a plus for web marketing companies and in a global marketplace.

Though there are advantages to having your virtual office near you, and a lot of areas have them, if you need meeting space, some local vendors offer that as an extra service. Some of your clients may like seeing a familiar address on your business materials. The website hq.com is a good place to find local meeting places and virtual offices.

Your virtual staff talent pool is huge. Many online companies and freelance vendors provide these services.

You can have an executive address. If you do business out of your home, having a business address looks better than a home address. You can use the professional address on all of your business materials and your website. Working from home is a good way to start a business, and even to continue one forever. But you might not want your customers to know that. A virtual office in Brunswick, Georgia, which I found through Davinci, for instance, offers a prime business address, mail and package receipt, business support center, lobby greeter, client drop-off/pickup, lobby directory listing, mail forwarding and shipping, conference room, and a daytime office. The same thing is offered all over the United States. This service started at about $85 a month.

You can hire a live receptionist to screen and transfer calls. They can take orders, schedule appointments, fax, and e-mail. You can also hire some of these services to be automated, which is cheaper. Of course, a machine can't do what a live receptionist can. It depends on your needs.

Some Disadvantages

Not everything is perfect in the virtual world. However, savvy business people can avoid some problems by drawing up tight, specific contracts they will use to employ virtual vendors. A large, experienced company with an established online reputation may have taken care of problems already. Virtual assistants need to assure you that they work with high standards to reduce concerns of quality and validity. Confidentiality and protection of your business's precious data should be of great concern to them—and you.

Technology problems can interrupt a meeting or online chat. And log-in problems can be disruptive for remote conferences. According to an article in ehow.com, "Businesses have to be diligent in ensuring that the technology remote workers use is functional and is a priority to their IT department." The article goes on to say that supervisors have to learn to assess performance based on results. You need to be sure your employees can do the best job for you, no matter where they are.

Management and workers need to be very organized for a virtual office to succeed. This can be done when you treat virtual staff as you would regular staff. Setting definite deadlines for task assignments, speaking to vendors daily, and using regular progress reports can help ensure tasks are being done in a timely manner. Therefore, it's important to train your virtual staff about the needs of your company. When they have a thorough knowledge of what you expect and what your company hopes to accomplish, your virtual staff can work better. They can also feel they are part of a team working to fulfill your goals. Above all, keep an open (virtual) door so you can address any concerns. Don't make it hard for your virtual employees to ask questions because you're unavailable. E-mail is an efficient way to handle all of your necessary communication. And, it can be even better than face-to-face instructions; employees can forget conversations, but they can always refer back to written e-mail instructions.

Step-by-Step Setup for Your Virtual Office

If you've decided a virtual office will work best for you, the following should help you take the steps needed to get started.

Put Your Plan on Paper

Write out your company goals before you decide precisely what you need. A business plan is always good for business, even virtual ones. Don't skip this step. Business plans are not just for seeking funding. Plans are made from goals, so be sure what your goals are. You need at least two, maybe three, columns for this. Start-up plans and goals come first, then perhaps six-month goals and maybe goals for one year later. Include start-up money and money needed for growth.

This is the time to decide if you need a virtual assistant who specializes in office setup. A VA can help you with your plans and also manage the office after the plans are in place. This is also the time to decide what VOPs and auxiliary support you need to hire. Do you need a live receptionist or an automated answering system? Do you need immediate marketing? If so, what kind? Do you need a website now or can that wait until later? And, finally, do you need physical office workers as well as virtual ones or can everything be handled virtually?

Purchase Your Equipment

If you want to be portable, get a laptop computer and not a desktop. Or, another device, such as a smartphone, may handle some of your needs remotely. If you're using a laptop, all of your files will go wherever you go. For whatever computer type you choose, you need enough hard drive and memory space to run several programs at once and a fast processor. Choose software and an antivirus program for the computer based on your work needs and what communication methods you plan to use.

This is another area where a VA can help you make a decision. For laptops, you may need a portable Internet device, which you can sometimes get through your cell phone provider; just make sure it can travel to the places you will be going. All other office equipment needs—such as printers and fax machines—are relative to the type of business you're in, and some virtual office providers offer these services, so you may not need to buy the equipment.

Choose a Business Address

You can use your own home address or rent an address in order to be totally virtual. Prices to rent an address start at about $80 per month, with setup fees of around $100. Included in this are mail pick-up and a prestigious address. On the more expensive end, for several hundred dollars a month, you can get packages, such as those offered through regus.com that include phone answering and mail services in one package.

As mentioned above, Mailbox Forwarding is another service that can handle your mail and give you an address to receive it. This service receives your mail or package and can forward it to you or scan it so you can view the contents online and then shred and recycle the mail. Prices for this company start at approximately $15 per month.

Decide if You Need Receptionist Services

Someone has to answer your phones if you don't do it yourself. If you don't rent an office location that provides phone services, there are many other online options. Davinci Virtual offers phone-answering services starting around $100 per month. Office Scape, with starting fees about $180 a month, includes a receptionist and business address in one package. CallRuby.com has a variety of receptionist packages, ranging from $209 to $699 per month, depending on minutes bought, voicemail boxes, and talk time.

If you don't want to hire an online receptionist, call your local phone company and ask if they have phone systems with IVR (interactive voice response) technology, which can help manage calls without you being on-site. Or, you can use a PBX system through TalkSwitch.com or VirtualPBX.com. PBX stands for private branch exchange and operates like an old-fashioned switchboard. Virtual PBX gives you the option of auto-response or live-answering from one of your employees. Conference calls are included.

Decide if You Need Physical Space for Meetings

Davinci Virtual offers physical offices to rent all over the United States. In Eatontown, New Jersey, for instance, you can rent space for $10–$35 per hour and conference space for $25–$40 per hour. It comes as part of a larger package starting at $100 per month. Intelligent Office offers 16 hours of office-space time with its package that includes address, mail service, phone answering, etc., starting around $280 per month, with a set-up fee of about $200.

Decide if Your Business Will Need Web Conferencing

If e-mail and instant messaging aren't enough for your contacts and you want to involve more people, web conferencing is the way to go, and there are many web conferencing tools to work with. Web conferencing is the online equivalent of a group meeting, according to Michael Miller in his book *Cloud Computing* (Que, 2008). Instead of having a one-to-one conversation, it is a one-to-many or many-to-many conversation.

Typically, each participant sits at his own computer and is connected via the Internet to the other conference members. For instance, it can be a one-way communication, as in a PowerPoint presentation. Or, it can be two-way, where each person shows his own content to the others. You can share applications, documents, whiteboard, and text-based chat. Some web conference providers charge a monthly or annual fee, while others charge a per-minute or pay-per-use rate. A few web conferencing hosts are Glance, Adobe Acrobat Connect, GotoMeeting, and Webex.

Ask for a Trial Run

Whether you choose to hire freelancers individually or through an online provider, ask for a trial run. If you don't understand the virtual services that are offered, ask questions until you are satisfied. Be specific. During your trial run, judge the work by how it will sound or look to your customers. During this trial run, communicate your confidentiality needs and have a specifically signed agreement available; evaluate how well the virtual employees understand and adhere to your confidentiality standards.

Decide How Your Employees Will Submit Invoices

Virtual assistance services and packagers will handle the invoicing if you go that route. But if you choose to hire freelancers on your own, you will need to agree on payment and invoicing plans.

Guidelines for Choosing Assistants for Your Company

Here are nine points you should use to judge the competency of virtual office personnel you may want to hire. All these items apply, whether you're hiring freelancers individually or working through an agency.

1. **Website presence:** Does a virtual assistant candidate have a website that projects a professional image? Check the VA's goals, ethics, or values to make sure they match yours. Look for typos, sloppy writing, misspellings, bad grammar, and formatting problems. Is the information coherent? If you are checking out a service provider such as Davinci, the company website may be all you can see, but they are professionals and can anticipate your questions and concerns.
2. **Personal presentation:** Whether you're finding someone on your own or through an online agency, you should be able to virtually "meet" your potential employee and have a phone conversation. Does she answer your concerns? Does he speak professionally? Is she prompt for the meeting time? If choosing someone who works freelance, ask questions specific to your business goals.
3. **Expertise:** You need someone with excellent business sense. Your virtual assistant needs both the know-how and the skills to care for your business and help it grow. Make sure your goals and values match. Ask questions, such as how many companies he has helped. What did he do to facilitate growth for those firms? Does he understand your company, what you do, etc., from his experience with similar businesses?
4. **Dependability and responsibility:** Is she dependable? Does he ask a lot of smart questions about your business? Does she initiate questions? Does he listen well? Can she articulate her questions and the answers she gives to yours? Do you feel you can trust him and would enjoy working with him?
5. **Experience:** A VA should have at least three to five years experience performing administrative tasks. Anyone can call themselves a VA. But that doesn't mean they meet the high standards of the industry. Ask specifics about a potential hire's experience using certain skills that you know you are going to need. For example, if you need someone who knows how to use auto-responders or HTML, be specific in finding someone who can handle those functions. Does the candidate understand business skills and operations? What are his strengths? The information on a candidate's website and marketing materials will serve as a résumé to you. Also ask if the candidate can provide references from current or former clients.

6. **Knowledge:** Experience is best for learning this job, but a good VA also needs to keep current on new trends and skills. Don't put too much weight on certification. Pay more attention to a candidate's professional manner and demeanor and how she demonstrates her qualifications through answers to your questions.
7. **Commitment to you:** You want someone who wants to serve your needs and expectations and is committed to your business and to pleasing you. Don't pick someone who just occasionally works this job or is just doing this until something better comes along. Ask how long he has been in business. Is she working full-time or part-time? Is this a chosen profession or a side job? Do his business standards match yours?
8. **References:** A serious professional will have references and testimonials on a personal website. If the candidate doesn't have a website, ask for references as you would if you were hiring traditionally.
9. **Pricing:** The average rates for a VA range from $30–$70 per hour. Expect to pay the same if hiring freelance workers. Fees from an online service will vary and may not be hourly, but may be a flat fee based on hours of service delivered per month. Don't choose someone just because of cheaper rates. As a seasoned businessperson, you know that quality and experience come at a price. Low rates could signal a lack of business sense and skill. It also means the candidate may be a risky investment. Low rates may make her take on more clients than she can handle, resulting in doing a poor job for you. You don't want to take the chance on inconsistent quality, delivery, and work. You want skill and compatibility. You will get great customer service from someone who cares about his work, and who's going to be around to finish it.

Straight Talk from Bob

Business gurus are fond of saying, "Work smarter—not harder."

But I don't know … I think there is something to be said for hard work.

Assuming you and I work equally smart, I'd think whichever one of us worked harder would come out ahead.

Hard work is good for what ails you.

When your business or job isn't going the way you want it to, buckle down and redouble your efforts. You'll be more productive, and at least some of your extra efforts will be rewarded—and hard work will have saved the day.

Goethe wrote, "Whoever strenuously endeavors, him we can rescue."

Combine hard work with persistence—never give up—and the odds of you getting the result you want increase geometrically.

Ironically, a lot of people who work hard like to pretend that they don't.

A famous Internet marketer, in promoting his programs, boasts about how you can make a six-figure income in Internet marketing with hardly any work. But I happen to know that this guy works at least 12 hours a day, six days a week—and often late into the night.

A famous copywriter is pictured lounging in his pool in a magazine profile of him. Yet, he seems to be continually at his PC, banging out successful ad after successful ad for his clients.

Most things that are worth having or achieving require hard work. If they were easy, everyone would have them.

Hard work alone does not guarantee success. You also have to work smart, of course.

But if you are not willing to put your nose to the grindstone, your chances of failure are large indeed. If you're not willing to do that, then there's not much chance you will be able to establish a successful home-based business, no matter how much you know or who you know or how good your marketing plan is.

You've now finished this book and your head is swimming with ideas. Now get ready for the hard part. Things not taking off as quickly as you want?

Work twice as hard. You may well get twice the results.

Resources

Want to learn more about any of the topics discussed in the book? Here are some ideas about where to start, with suggested websites, books, newsletters, and other material for many subjects, broken down by chapters.

Chapter 2: Home-Based Business Opportunity #1: Freelancing

On the Web:

SurveyMonkey, www.surveymonkey.com. Start with this company to see what's involved in doing the technical side of online surveys.

FreelanceSwitch, freelanceswitch.com. Community of expert freelancers from around the world. Site includes job board and directory, blog, forums, and more.

American Writers and Artists, Inc. (AWAI), www.awaionline.com. Offerings include programs in graphic design, self publishing, Internet marketing, resume writing, travel writing, photography and many more.

Small Business Administration (SBA), www.sba.gov. One-stop shopping for all kinds of information, including, but not limited to, creating a business plan, obtaining licenses, filing and paying taxes.

Entrepreneur, www.entrepreneur.com. This magazine and website covers different types of businesses and entrepreneurial ventures.

On the shelves:

How to Write & Sell Simple Information for Fun and Profit: Your Guide to Writing and Publishing Books, E-Books, Articles, Special Reports, Audio Programs, DVDs, and Other How-To Content by Robert W. Bly (Quill Driver Books, 2010)

Secrets of a Freelance Writer: How to Make $100,000 a Year or More by Robert W. Bly (Holt, 2006)

The Well-Fed Writer: Financial Self-Sufficiency as a Commercial Freelancer in Six Months or Less by Peter Bowerman (Fanove, 2009)

Chapter 3: Home-Based Business Opportunity #2: Consulting

On the Web:

Consultant Journal, www.consultantjournal.com/how-to-become-a-consultant. Information ranging from who hires consultants to how to determine your fee.

Entrepreneur, www.entrepreneur.com/article/41384. Includes list of 20 areas where consultants are thriving.

Business Consulting Buzz, www.consulting-business.com/. Started by cousins with worldwide business experience.

On the shelves:

Flawless Consulting: A Guide to Getting Your Expertise Used by Peter Block (Jossey-Bass Pfeiffer, 1981, reprinted 2000)

The Consulting Bible: Everything You Need to Know to Create and Expand a Seven-Figure Consulting Practice by Alan Weiss (Wiley and Sons, 2011)

Chapter 4: Home-Based Business Opportunity #3: Coaching

On the Web:

Passion for Business, www.passionforbusiness.com. This is a good place to start learning about coaching and what's involved in the endeavor, particularly for business coaching.

Behavioral Coaching Institute, www.1to1coachingschool.com. First international professional coach training institution specializing in executive coaching.

The Coaches Corner, www.howtoplay.com/coaches-corner-how-to-play.html. Information on coaching football and other sports, as well as motivational coaching.

Top Coaching Techniques, www.topcoachingtechniques.com. Life coaching techniques and programs.

Dale Carnegie Training Programs, www.dalecarnegie.com. Working since 1912 to help clients sharpen skills and improve their performance.

Worldwide Association of Business Coaches, www.wabccoaches.com. International association dedicated to the leadership and development of business coaching worldwide.

International Association of Coaching (IAC), www.certifiedcoach.org. The brainchild of Thomas J. Leonard, who is often credited as the founder of the modern coaching profession.

On the shelves:

Becoming a Professional Life Coach: Lessons from the Institute of Life Coach Training by Patrick Williams and Diane S. Menendez (Norton, 2007)

Chapter 5: Home-Based Business Opportunity #4: Selling On eBay

On the Web:

eBay, pages.ebay.com/help/sell/sell-getstarted.html. Nothing like getting information straight from the source.

wikiHow, www.wikihow.com/Sell-on-eBay. Whether you're a home-based business or just trying to sell some stuff you may have sitting around, here is a comprehensive guide to becoming an eBay seller.

Dummies.com, www.dummies.com/how-to/internet/ebay.html. Website for the "for Dummies" book series of books has a wealth of information, including special content for seniors.

Money Crashers, www.moneycrashers.com/ebay-selling-tips-maximize-profits/. Ten tips to increase your bottom line.

On the shelves:

eBay 101: Selling on eBay For Part-time or Full-time Income by Steve Weber (Weber Books, 2011)

Chapter 6: Home-Based Business Opportunity #5: Internet Marketing

On the Web:

Bob Bly, bly.com. Copywriting and Internet marketing advice.

On the shelves:

Internet Marketing Methods Revealed: The Complete Guide to Becoming an Internet Marketing Expert by Miguel Todaro (Atlantic Publishing Group, 2007)

Internet Marketing from the Real Experts by The Gang of 88, Shawn Collins and Missy Ward (Morgan James Publishing, 2010)

Chapter 7: Home-Based Business Opportunity #6: Close-Outs

On the Web:

Closeouts Central, www.closeouts-central.com. General close-out products include sneakers, shoes, apparel, cosmetics, baby merchandise, housewares, bedding and electronics.

GovDeals, www.Govdeals.com. An online auction marketplace for discontinued or surplus items from state, county, and city organizations, including schools and public utility groups.

Government Liquidation, www.govliquidation.com. The exclusive contractor of the Defense Logistics Agency Disposition Services for the sale of surplus and scrap assets of the United States Department of Defense.

Liquidation, www.liquidation.com. A well-known liquidation company handling businesses closing down and selling out their remaining inventory and other assets. Also partners with several government wholesale groups.

Merchandise USA, Inc., www.merchandiseusa.com. Check out the schedule of upcoming trade shows the company's buyers attend.

Shopster, www.shopster.com. Free network that lets you build an online store, connect to other merchants and suppliers, find drop ship products to sell, and also sell your own products through these new channels.

Wholesale EZ, www.wholesaleez.com. Provides a place to publicize your information if you are doing close-outs.

Wholesale Merchandise, www.thecloseoutnews.com. Provides information about what's selling and who is selling.

CHAPTER 8: HOME-BASED BUSINESS OPPORTUNITY #7: IMPORT/EXPORT

ON THE WEB:

MadeInChina.com, www.madeinchina.com. A well-known portal for wholesale merchandise from China. This site lists inventory in just about any category you can imagine.

Wholesalers Network, www.wholesalersnetwork.com. Go to this site to find merchandise and suppliers by country.

Liquidity Services, Inc., www.liquidityservicesinc.com. An international governmental online auction portal for selling items to other countries.

American Association of Exporters and Importers, www.aaei.org. Offers information, education, and advocacy on the part of importers and exporters.

Informed Trade International Import/Export, www.itintl.com. Offers resources for importers and exporters.

USAExportImport, www.usaexportimport.com. A variety of resources for both exporters and importers.

ON THE SHELVES:

Mastering Import & Export Management by Thomas Cook and Kelly Raia (AMACOM, 2012)

Chapter 9: Home-Based Business Opportunity #8: Real Estate

On the Web:

National Association of Realtors, www.realtor.org. America's largest trade association, representing over one million members involved in the residential and commercial real estate industries.

AIR Commercial Real Estate Association, www.airea.com. Association of industrial and office real estate brokerage professionals dedicated to providing information, industry standards, services, and education.

NAIOP, www.naiop.org. One of North America's largest commercial real estate organizations.

The Appraisal Foundation, www.appraisalfoundation.org. Organization dedicated to promoting professionalism and ensuring public trust in the valuation profession.

Institute of Real Estate Management, www.irem.org. Trade association providing education and information for the property manager. Affiliate of the National Association of Realtors.

Society of Industrial and Office Realtors, www.sior.com. Professional commercial and industrial real estate association.

On the shelves:

Sell with Soul: Creating an Extraordinary Career in Real Estate Without Losing Your Friends, Your Principles or Your Self-Respect by Jennifer Allan (BlueGreen Books, 2008)

Chapter 10: Launching Your New Business

On the Web:

Grants.gov, www.grants.gov. Take a look at this site to see if there is anything you can apply for in your niche. It's always nice to get money that you don't have to pay back!

FindLaw, smallbusiness.findlaw.com. FindLaw's Small Business Center provides information and resources for small business owners and help for entrepreneurs seeking to get a business idea off the ground.

BusinessNameUSA, www.businessnameusa.com. Provides information about creating and registering a business name and getting your business off the ground.

ON THE SHELVES:

The Everything Start Your Own Business Book: New and Updated Strategies for Running a Successful Business by Judith B. Harrington (Adams Media Corp., 2012)

Start Your Own Business, Fifth Edition: The Only Start-Up Book You'll Ever Need (Entrepreneur Press, 2010)

CHAPTER 11: SETTING UP A HOME OFFICE

ON THE WEB:

HGTV, www.hgtv.com/topics/home-office/index.html. Lots of good tips and videos on a variety of topics.

Houzz.com, www.houzz.com/photos/home-office. For inspiration, check out these photos of dream setups.

About.com, interiordec.about.com/od/planninganoffice/a/budgethomeoffic.htm. Tips for setting up an office on a budget.

ON THE SHELVES:

The Smarter Home Office: 8 Simple Steps To Increase Your Income, Inspiration and Comfort by Linda Varone (Grant Meadows Publishing, 2010)

CHAPTER 12: MARKETING AND PROMOTING YOUR NEW BUSINESS

ON THE WEB:

Pagemodo, www.pagemodo.com. Helps create a starter welcome page for your business account on Facebook. Although it's an external application, you will link through to Facebook. Make sure your business side of the Facebook account is already set up first!

Nick Usborne, www.nickusborne.com. Nick created AWAI's Social Media Expert program, which is a good course to take when you barely know anything other than the basics of Facebook and Twitter. Go to www.awaionline.com to sign up for the Social Media Expert program.

HubSpot, www.hubspot.com. Sign up for this newsletter to keep in touch with the latest and greatest of the Internet and social media practices.

MW Strategic Marketing, www.mwstrategicmarketing.com. Specializes in providing small business marketing resources, help, consulting, and coaching services.

Marketing Consultants Inc, www.marketingrecruiters.com. An executive search firm specializing in recruiting marketing professionals on a nationwide basis that makes successful matches between clients and candidates.

Constant Contact, www.constantcontact.com. Tools to build strong connections with clients and reach new customers.

ON THE SHELVES:

The Best of Guerrilla Marketing—Guerrilla Marketing Remix by Jay Conrad Levinson and Jeannie Levinson (Entrepreneur Press, 2011)

The Marketing Plan Handbook: Develop Big-Picture Marketing Plans for Pennies on the Dollar by Robert W. Bly (Entrepreneur Press, 2010)

Ultimate Guide to Facebook Advertising: How to Access 600 Million Customers in 10 Minutes by Perry Marshall and Thomas Meloche (Entrepreneur Press, 2011)

CHAPTER 13: BECOMING A THOUGHT LEADER IN YOUR NICHE

ON THE WEB:

Small Business Trends, www.smallbiztrends.com/2012/10/become-an-expert-online.html. Online publication for small business owners, entrepreneurs, and the people who interact with them.

Small Business Association, www.sba.gov/community/blogs/guest-blogs/industry-word/how-become-industry-expert. Blogger gives lots of ideas of how to get your name in front of people.

ON THE SHELVES:

Becoming a Recognized Authority in Your Field in 60 Days or Less! by Robert W. Bly (Alpha, 2002)

Becoming THE Expert: Enhancing Your Business Reputation Through Thought Leadership Marketing by John Hayes (Brightword, 2012)

Thought Leadership: Moving Hearts and Minds by Robin Ryde (Palgrave Macmillan, 2007)

CHAPTER 14: OPERATING AS A VIRTUAL COMPANY

ON THE WEB:

Virtual Assistant Career Guide, virtualassistantcareerguide.com. Filled with good, solid information about starting your own virtual assistant business from home.

Intelligent Office, intelligentoffice.com. Offers an array of virtual office services.

OfficeScape, officescape.com. Office service and technology provider.

Regus, regus.com. Provides "flexible" work spaces to companies worldwide.

Mailbox Forwarding, mailboxforwarding.com. Provides you with a mailing address that is accessible online, where you can receive and view all your mail—letters, documents, and packages, whether delivered by the USPS, FedEx, or UPS.

Administrative Consultant's Association, virtualassistantnetworking.com. Online professional community and education resource just for administrative experts.

ON THE SHELVES:

Encyclopedia of Small Business, Vol. 2, 3rd ed. (Gale, 2007)

Start Your Own Net Services Business by Entrepreneur Press and Liane Cassavoy (Entrepreneur Media, 2009)

Index

About the Author

Bob Bly is an Internet marketer and copywriter with more than 30 years of experience in business-to-business and direct marketing. McGraw-Hill calls Bob Bly "America's top copywriter" and AWAI named him its 2007 Copywriter of the Year. His clients include IBM, the Conference Board, PSE&G, AT&T, Ott-Lite Technology, Intuit, ExecuNet, Boardroom, Medical Economics, Grumman, RCA, ITT Fluid Technology, and Praxair.

Bob is also an active Internet information marketer, having started his Internet marketing business at age 48. His online sales average $1,000 a day from more than five dozen websites, and his e-list has over 65,000 subscribers. For his work in Internet marketing, Bob has won a Standard of Excellence Award from the Web Marketing Association and the Lifetime Marketing Achievement Award from "Early to Rise," a daily e-newsletter with over 450,000 subscribers.

Bob is the author of more than 75 books, including *Selling Your Services* (Henry Holt), *The Elements of Business Writing* (Alyn & Bacon), and *How to Write & Sell Simple Information for Fun and Profit* (Quill Driver Books). Bob's articles have appeared in *Cosmopolitan*, *Writer's Digest*, *Successful Meetings*, *Amtrak Express*, *Direct*, and many other publications, and he writes regular columns for *The Writer* and *Target Marketing*.

Bob's awards include a Gold Echo from the Direct Marketing Association, an IMMY from the Information Industry Association, two Southstar Awards, and an American Corporate Identity Award of Excellence. He is a member of the Specialized Information Publishers Association (SIPA), American Institute of Chemical Engineers (AIChE), and Business Marketing Association (BMA).

Questions and comments may be sent to:

Bob Bly
CTC Publishing
590 Delcina Drive
River Vale, NJ 07675
Phone 201-505-9451
E-mail: rwbly@bly.com
Web: www.bly.com